THE SPIRIT
AND THE LETTER

THE SPIRIT
AND THE LETTER
The Struggle for
Rights in America

BERNICE KOHN

THE VIKING PRESS NEW YORK

For Morton, my mentor — and more

LIBRARY OF CONGRESS CATALOGING IN PUBLICATION DATA

Hunt, Bernice Kohn. The spirit and the letter. SUMMARY:
Discusses the first ten amendments, the concepts on which
they were based, and the interpretations drawn from them
through a series of test cases. 1. Civil rights — United States —
Juvenile literature. 2. United States. Constitution. 1st–10th
amendments — Juvenile literature. [1. Civil rights. 2. United
States. Constitution. 1st–10th amendments] I. Title.
KF4750.H85   342'.73'085   73–22306
ISBN 0–670–66301–8

PICTURE CREDITS

Danny Lyon © 1968 Magnum Photos, jacket, 104; Culver
Pictures, 8; The Granger Collection, 16; United Press Inter-
national, 34; Wide World Photos, 48; Fred Ward from Black
Star, 66; New York Times/Mike Lien, 76; Don Rutledge from
Black Star, 90; Burt Glinn © 1970 Magnum Photos, 120.

Contents

I have a dream that one day this nation will rise up and live out the true meaning of its creed . . .

DR. MARTIN LUTHER KING, JR.

Since we live on earth, not in Heaven, we will always be imperfect. Yet in spite of all obstacles, the creation of a Bill of Rights marks a start toward achieving a society where diversities in ideas, as well as race, can exist and flourish side by side. A Bill of Rights sets the ideal to which on occasion the people can be summoned. It is a reminder to officials that all power is a heady thing and that there are limits beyond which it is not safe to go.

JUSTICE WILLIAM O. DOUGLAS

Reading the Declaration of Independence to the public

The
Birth of
a Nation

ONE FINE DAY in spring, about two hundred years ago, Mr. Thomas Jefferson, age 33, arrived in Philadelphia astride a smart-looking, briskly trotting horse. He had ridden up from his home in Monticello, Virginia, to take his seat at the Continental Congress, a gathering of representatives from thirteen very angry colonies.

The men and women who lived in the American colonies had strong beliefs in freedom and the personal rights of all men. Such ideals were founded in the ancient Greek, Jewish, and finally Christian traditions — that each individual had been created by God in His image, endowed with dignity as a person, and entitled to *live* in dignity and freedom. One of the reasons the colonists had left their homeland and come to a wilderness was in order to live according to their beliefs.

Nowhere in the Europe these people had fled was there more awareness of civil rights than in England. As long ago as the year 1215, King John, at Runnymede, had signed the Magna Carta. For the first time in history a British king had admitted (albeit grudgingly) that he did not hold absolute power over his subjects. Feudal barons and other nobles were granted some rights.

And later, rights even filtered down to the common people. In 1689, a British Bill of Rights made certain guarantees to Britons; they included the rights to freedom of speech and of elections, to trial by jury, and to freedom from cruel and unusual punishments such as burning or other forms of torture.

But in spite of these rights, the Puritans had left England, first for Holland and then America, because of what they considered Roman corruption within the Church of England. Such remnants of Catholicism as bishops, ecclesiastical courts, altars and vestments, as well as the practice of kneeling, all seemed contrary to the word of God. The Puritans became strong dissenters within the church and were finally outlawed from it and persecuted as revolutionaries. They left England not only to flee the law, but because along with other freedoms, these people wanted full freedom to worship in their own fashion, and they were willing to give up their homes and their country to have it.

The Puritans were young, they were determined, they coped with enormous hardships in their first years in the primitive commune they called Plymouth Colony. Supplies from England failed to arrive and although the colony ultimately learned to be self-supporting, many of its members died in the process. With such sacrifices in their background, these people would not easily settle for anything less than freedom.

Another influence on the determination of the Puritans was the philosophy of John Locke. His two treatises on civil government, published in 1689 and 1690, dealt with what Locke termed natural laws, and they were familiar to every educated American. The central idea was that man gave up the simple state of nature and submitted to civil government for the sole purpose of protecting his natural rights. Locke believed that all men were free, independent, and equal, and that no man could be subjected to the political power of another unless he consented to do so. The main purpose of a government was to protect the life, liberty, and property of the people, and any government that failed in this task deserved to be changed or overthrown by the people.

In addition, certain ideas of civil liberty were shared by all Englishmen, and although an ocean separated them from the British Isles, the colonists were *English*. They were entitled to, and expected, the same rights as other Englishmen. Imagine, then, their outrage when King George III came to the throne in 1760 and raised the taxes of the colonists while denying them representatives in Parliament. Such a thing was unheard of. The cry of "No taxation without representation," which rang throughout the land, soon became a battle cry. A full-scale revolution for independence from the king was under way.

The way was not easy, and it was June 7, 1776, before the rebels declared themselves to be "free and independent states." So far, however, they had declared it only to themselves, and it seemed necessary to make a formal declaration to the king and to the rest of the world. To this end, the new Congress appointed a committee of five men to draw up a document.

One of the five was Thomas Jefferson, and since he was known to have a flair for writing, the task of composition fell to him. Jefferson made himself as comfortable as possible in the parlor on the second floor of a bricklayer's house, then labored over his task during two weeks of a sweltering Philadelphia summer. It was not only the heat that bothered him. There was something less than peace and harmony within the committee, and indeed within the Congress. One major problem was Jefferson's belief that there was no place for slavery in the new nation (although Jefferson himself, with a large plantation to maintain and no other feasible way to maintain it, continued to own slaves throughout his lifetime!). Almost a third of the population were slaves, and this certainly did not fit the ideals of a people dedicated to liberty, dignity, and freedom. Jefferson took pains to say so in his first draft of the Declaration, but the disapproval of most of the First Continental Congress was so great that he was forced to strike out the passage.

There were other arguments, too, but finally, all changes made, the Declaration of Independence was approved by Congress on July 4, 1776. The men who had framed it knew full well that, under British law, they were now guilty of treason. They could lose their lives for this piece of paper, which said in part:

We hold these Truths to be self-evident, that all men are created equal, that they are endowed by their Creator with certain unalienable Rights, that among these are Life, Liberty, and the Pursuit of Happiness — That to secure these Rights, Governments are instituted among Men, deriving their just powers from the Consent of the Governed, that whenever any Form of Government becomes destructive of these Ends, it is the Right of the People to alter or to abolish it, and to institute new Government.

Noble and beautiful words to be sure, and a poetic beginning for a new nation. The best of all possible worlds? Perhaps, but this was only a statement of belief and intent. An introduction, at best, to a book that was yet to be written. A constitution still had to be drafted, a body of laws created. The founding fathers knew that. What they could *not* have foreseen was that two hundred years later, we would still be laboring to perfect what they had just begun.

We the People

The Constitution of the United States of America

THE FIRST YEARS were difficult, very nearly impossible. There were still Loyalists devoted to the English king who had to be subdued. There were disagreements within the churches on ritual and other religious matters — for as often happens, the same people who were in perfect accord on what they *didn't* like in the Church of England had different ideas of what was right and proper in America.

Most important of all, there was strong conflict over the question of slavery. Although the Declaration had stated that "all men are created equal," slavery was a fact. Most of the states did pass laws (which continued to be broken) forbidding the further importation of slaves, but few Northerners and almost no Southerners freed the slaves they already owned. This failure to combine principle with practice is one that we are still paying for dearly.

In spite of the fact that this was a rebellious and unusually young population — in 1776 half the people were under sixteen, and three-fourths were under twenty-five — the early Americans were far from democratic by our standards. Although there was no aristocracy as in Europe, social and political power were largely the privilege of sizable property-owners. The war had served to level things to some degree since many of the wealthy lost their holdings due to the British trade blockade, and many poor farmers grew rich by selling supplies to the army. But the difference between rich and poor was still dramatic.

By March, 1781, the Articles of Confederation at last loosely joined the Thirteen Colonies into a single body, but the problems facing the new nation were so overwhelming that the future did not look at all promising.

The war dragged on and General Washington tried mightily, but in vain, to give courage and hope to his ragged troops as he led them against the British forces. The colonists had been soundly beaten at the Battle of Camden only a half year before and hadn't yet recovered from the blow. At the end of a long, hard winter, the soldiers were cold, hungry, weary, and thoroughly discouraged. To make matters worse, there was no longer any money for their pay, and they complained and grumbled more each day. The outlook was totally grim. Soon, however, the balance was about to shift, and by October, General Cornwallis would be forced to surrender. But there was no hint of the coming victory in March.

Like the soldiers, the individual states were discontented and uneasy. There was enormous jealousy and rivalry among them over land territories. They were also constantly quarreling over matters of trade and border taxes. Lacking a central government (except for Congress) or any form of federal taxation, the states had to resort to any means possible whenever funds were needed. Most of the states set up complicated systems of taxation that were different from those of their neighboring states. The result was that practically every time a citizen crossed a state border to sell a hog or to buy a bolt of cloth, he had to pay a tax of one sort or another. Most of the taxes were excessive, and the citizen, understandably, became angry.

While the end of the war brought a temporary lift of spirits, it didn't solve any of the basic problems. In fact, without the need to act together against a common enemy, the states became even more involved with their own affairs and more concerned with their own powers. They paid little or no attention to Congress, refusing to send funds as requested, and often not even bothering to send men to represent them. When they did take the trouble to send representatives, the congressmen frequently arrived days or even weeks after they were expected.

Congress was powerless to do anything about any of this since the Articles of Confederation had given it only the right to resolve or to recommend, but not the right to enforce. It had no courts, no authority to implement taxation, no control over trade. The weakness was so critical that it quickly became quite clear that without a strong central government the new United States could not long remain united.

On February 21, 1787, the now desperate Congress approved a plan for a convention in Philadelphia to revise the Articles of Confederation. Drastic action would be needed to consolidate the bickering states and to ease the economic and spiritual depressions of the young nation. As things stood, several European nations were eyeing the situation with interest, and the danger of an invasion from the Continent was very real. There was also a growing possibility of revolution by the increasingly discontented poor people, a group we would think of today as the early American political left wing.

The Convention officially opened on May 14, 1787, but many delegates straggled to Philadelphia at a leisurely pace. In time, representatives of twelve states — Rhode Island flatly refused to take part — arrived at the Pennsylvania State House, now known as Independence Hall. They met in the same room where eight of the group had signed the Declaration of Independence eleven years earlier.

Among the delegates assembled in the handsome red brick building were George Washington, Benjamin Franklin, Alexander Hamilton, James Madison, and Gouverneur Morris. Washington, with his martial bearing, cut an impressive figure. By contrast, the eighty-one-year-old Benjamin Franklin, suffering acutely from gout, attracted attention when he arrived in a sedan chair borne by four prisoners "on leave" for the occasion from the Walnut Street jail. Gouverneur Morris must have aroused some interest, too, as he clomped around on his wooden leg.

Whatever the intention of Congress in calling the Convention, its course was set when Governor Randolph of Virginia presented a fifteen-point plan designed *not* to revise the old Articles, but rather to establish a completely new form of government. There was furious debate over the so-called Virginia Plan, and almost as much over the New Jersey Plan, which attempted to modify it.

By July, the Convention agreed to drop both of the controversial plans and adopt one which became known, appropriately, as the Great Compromise.

After a short vacation, the delegates returned to the East Room of the State House. They settled down at green cloth-covered tables and dug into the hard job at hand. The heat was sweltering, and the men often repaired to The Indian Queen, a nearby tavern, for cooling drinks.

Slavery was a major issue for debate, and it was clear from the outset that the cotton-producing South had very different problems from the North. Southerners claimed that without slaves they could not raise the cotton on which their economy depended, and therefore, they would not participate in a government that barred the slave trade. Eventually, compromises satisfactory to both sides were made, and by August, the men had worked out a first draft of the Constitution. It called for a Congress consisting of a House of Representatives and a Senate, a President of the United States, and a Supreme Court.

The final draft of the Constitution was ready in September, 1789. Like the convention delegates, the states found little ground for agreement but much for argument. The fights for ratification in the individual states raged for two and a half years. In 1790, the last straggler, Rhode Island, joined the Union and the task was completed.

Now the new nation had a central government. Moreover, and of prime importance to the liberty-loving founders, it had a Constitution that guaranteed certain civil rights and liberties to the citizens.

It should be pointed out here that there is no single, brief, and concise definition of civil rights. Basically, they are those rights to which a person is entitled by virtue of his citizenship; they protect the individual against the power of his government. Civil rights, as we know them, spring directly from Locke's concept of natural rights: all men are free, equal, entitled to life, liberty, property, and to change or overthrow the government if it fails to protect those rights.

Legal rights *include* civil rights, but they also protect the citizen against the wrongs of other individuals — or of groups of individuals, rather than the government alone.

Civil rights were not the rule throughout the world in the eighteenth century (nor are they yet), and the new Americans were aware of the importance of such liberties. Borrowing heavily from English tradition, the Constitution assured a writ of *habeas corpus* — a safeguard against illegal imprisonment. Among other protections, it also guaranteed trial by jury, provided safeguards to money in the treasury, eliminated titles of nobility, and declared that no religious test would ever be required of a person seeking public office.

In spite of this concern for rights in the Constitution, there were many who believed that it was too general and too meager. Many of the states felt that there should have been a specific Bill of Rights, and this was one of the reasons those states had taken so long to ratify the Constitution. Some of the states drew up their own bills which were included in the state constitutions, but of course they were valid only within the state to which each applied.

It was generally understood by the time the Constitution was adopted that a Bill of Rights would soon be added. And in fact, as soon as the first Congress met, in 1789, that was done. The bill was in the form of the first ten amendments, and by 1791, it was ratified by the necessary three-quarters of the states.

The Bill of Rights guaranteed that each American

could worship as he pleased, speak out publicly on any subject, and meet with others; it guarded against unreasonable search and seizure, and self-incrimination. It promised fair trial by jury, reasonable bail and punishment, and the right to legal counsel. It also granted the right of a citizen to keep silent under certain circumstances.

The Bill of Rights marked a beginning to rights amendments, but not an end. Five more were added in later years — six more if the Twenty-sixth Amendment, giving eighteen-year-olds the right to vote and ratified in 1971, is counted as a rights amendment. Doubtless, there will be others. The full text of the Constitution, with its amendments, appears at the back of this book.

A citizen of any totalitarian country reading the rights granted by the Constitution of the United States would be envious. Americans appear to be thoroughly protected. Nothing seems to have been overlooked. We are guaranteed many personal freedoms. The slaves were freed by the Thirteenth Amendment and made citizens by the Fourteenth; the latter amendment tells us that all citizens have equal protection of the laws. The Constitution even guards the rights of accused persons and promises them the protection of the laws and a fair trial.

In a totalitarian country, the government has a

legal right to jail a citizen for expressing an unpopular political opinion or for refusing to answer a question. Without the right of *habeas corpus*, he can be jailed simply on suspicion and kept in jail indefinitely, without a trial. If there is a trial, he may or may not have a lawyer, may never even learn who has accused him, and in an extreme case, may lose his life without having had the opportunity to defend himself in any way.

A visitor from an undemocratic country would be *right* to envy Americans — but he might also wonder why, with such a fine Constitution, the United States has had to strive and struggle for civil liberties. While social upheavals are nothing new in the United States, the violent ferment of the 1960's and 1970's seems particularly vivid because of its immediacy.

Americans might well be puzzled by the extraordinary number of demonstrations, riots, protests, and outbreaks of violence. Everyone talks about civil rights — but if they are written into the Constitution, how is it that we still have to fight for them? Are all Americans really equal? And if not, why aren't they? What rights do Americans have, and why is there any question about them?

The answers will fill the rest of this book, but one of the first things we must consider is the Constitution itself. It is written in broad terms which are often difficult to understand — not just for *you* to understand, but even for lawyers and judges. There are phrases in it such as "due process of law," "probable cause," "unreasonable searches," and "excessive bail." How much bail is excessive? A thousand dollars may seem little to a wealthy man and ten dollars excessive to a pauper.

Another problem within the Constitution is that the Bill of Rights, written by people whose recent experience had been with the power of a monarchy, was meant to protect the people against the power of *Federal* government. It did not apply to the states, and state courts did not have to pay any attention to it.

The Fourteenth Amendment, ratified in 1868, says in part, "No State shall . . . deprive any person of life, liberty, or property, without due process of law." This sounds as if it meant that the Bill of Rights had to be observed by the states, but it didn't work out that way automatically. It took the Supreme Court, decision by decision, to force the states to observe the Bill of Rights. Many of the decisions have been handed down rather recently.

Another difficulty is, simultaneously, a source of pride. On the one hand, our original Constitution, two centuries old and still in use, is admirable for its ideals. But on the other hand, two centuries is a great deal of time. It is doubtful that our Founding Fathers could have pictured a teeming, sprawling American city of today. A city with its large population, its factories, highways, schools, and housing; its complex economic problems and unemployment; overcrowded schools, poor health facilities; the growth of ghettos; the combination of unbearable pressures that accrued on less privileged people; the resulting spread of hopelessness, anger, crime; the need for large police forces, the many jails, and the courts with overcrowded calendars. To an eighteenth-century American — even one from the largest city, Colonial Philadelphia of green squares, flowing rivers, and checkerboard streets lined with red brick houses — all of this would surely have been beyond imagination.

It is surprising and impressive, then, that with such dramatic changes over the decades, our Constitution has remained so practical and relevant. One reason, of course, is that it can be amended; the other is its provision for a Supreme Court. Congress makes our laws, the President may veto them; but the Supreme Court, through a system of judicial review, decides which laws and which actions are in harmony with our Constitution and its ideals, and which are not. The Supreme Court *interprets* the Constitution, decides the meaning of those broad terms that the rest of us find so puzzling, and how they apply to contemporary conditions. Only the Supreme Court can say how much bail is "excessive," what punishment is "cruel and unusual." The Court is the supreme law of the land. It has changed and, hopefully, will continue to change the application of the Constitution to fit the needs of modern life.

We get a first clue to the importance of the Court from the imposing structure that houses it. The present Supreme Court building, in Washington, D.C., is modeled after the Temple of Diana at Ephesus, which was one of the seven wonders of the ancient world. The Courthouse, on Capitol Hill, is of gleaming white marble and has a stately facade of corinthian columns. Its bronze doors weigh over six tons each, and the ceiling of the courtroom soars to a height of forty-four feet. It is a building that projects an air of dignity and formality.

Within those walls, nine men in black robes — eight Justices and one Chief Justice — listen, confer, and decide. When the Chief Justice agrees with the majority, he appoints one of the Justices to write the opinion of the Court; when he does not agree with the majority, the ranking Justice of that group makes the appointment. In each case, all Justices are free to write their own concurring (agreeing) or dissenting (disagreeing) opinions.

The Court makes decisions only when it has been asked to and when it thinks its opinion is necessary. Rarely does a case *begin* in the Supreme Court; most often, it has been tried in all of the lower courts first. Then, if one of the parties believes that a question of constitutional law is involved and that he is actually endangered because of a misunderstanding of the law, he may ask the Supreme Court to review the case. The Supreme Court reviews only a small percentage of the cases that come to its attention, but once it makes a decision, that decision stand as the law of the land.

The Supreme Court can reverse any decision of a lower court and it can declare any law, either Federal or state, unconstitutional. That means that the law is in violation of the Constitution and cannot be permitted to stand. The Court has abolished hundreds of state laws in this way, and in so doing, has established a number of rights for Americans.

Since the Supreme Court has been in existence as long as the Constitution itself, it is reasonable to wonder why it took so long to establish some rights that seem basic. One reason is that Justices are people. Like all people, they are part of the society in which they live, and are sensitive to the feelings of that society. It has never been possible for any Supreme Court to make decisions which were *totally* beyond the beliefs of current society. Can you imagine, for example, what would have happened in Puritan America—or even Victorian America—if the Court had been asked to decide a case involving sex education in public schools? Almost surely, the Justices would not have considered such a program a matter of free speech or press, but rather an outrageous plot to defile children. The Justices would have been reflecting the almost universal belief of society at that time, that sex was dirty, dangerous, and not a thing for children to know about at all. Times change and so do beliefs.

Another influence on the decisions of each Justice is his own personal liberal or conservative, open-minded or narrow, point of view. High Court Justices are appointed by the president and may—but do not always—share the president's political opinions. Since Justices are appointed for life, the Court at any given time may be made up of men with widely differing views. Or, on the contrary, it may be largely conservative or largely liberal. Earl Warren was appointed Chief Justice of the Supreme Court by relatively conservative President Dwight D. Eisenhower in 1953. And although there were many changes in the Court before Warren resigned in

1969, the "Warren Court" is outstanding in the history of the nation for liberal decisions that contributed to the rights of Americans.

The flexibility of the Supreme Court and of the Constitution itself is of extreme importance. All law, although a body of rules enforced for the good of society, is actually an outgrowth of the customs of that society. What at first seems simply "right," "moral," or culturally or socially acceptable to the majority of the people, gradually becomes the law.

But mistakes occur. It sometimes happens that a law is passed and is so unpopular that it is virtually impossible for the states to enforce it. The Eighteenth Amendment, popularly known as Prohibition, was such a law; so many people broke it, that it became clear that it would have to be repealed. It was, by the Twenty-first Amendment.

The process of changing laws is what keeps our democracy alive. Every time the Supreme Court makes a decision under the Bill of Rights, it faces the problem of the rights of the individual against the rights of the entire society. For example, we are all entitled to free speech, but at the same time, it is the business of our laws to protect us against false or misleading advertising. It could be argued that it is a violation of the First Amendment to prohibit anyone from advertising a product guaranteed to grow hair on bald heads, to turn fat people into thin ones without diet, or to cure an incurable disease with a pill. Yet we generally agree that fraudulent claims should not be legal.

It seems to be an unfortunate fact that in a democracy, with many freedoms guaranteed, there are always a few people who, through greed, illness, or sheer perversity, prey upon others for gain. The Court must decide when to curb individual freedom in order to protect the rest of society.

It is through the action of the Court in making such decisions that the Bill of Rights has begun, at last, to have real meaning for modern Americans. The ways in which it has happened make for some interesting stories.

Conscientious objectors demonstrating against the war in Vietnam

The
Church and
the State

*Congress shall make no law respecting an establishment
of religion, or prohibiting the free exercise thereof...*
AMENDMENT I

As WE HAVE already seen, religion was an important matter for colonial Americans. It had been to gain religious freedom that they had left England in the first place, and above all things, they wanted to preserve that freedom in the United States. They intended to do it with the First Amendment.

But among the many phrases in the Constitution that have meant different things at different times, "establishment of religion," and "free exercise thereof" are outstanding. The definitions of those two terms have been debated in the courts again and again. Thomas Jefferson was of the opinion that the prohibition against an establishment of religion was meant "to build a wall of separation between Church and State." This was in defense against the system that prevailed in many European countries — including England — where there was an official state religion. Only one church was recognized, and those who did not belong to it were often shunned, punished, or even killed. A prime example of the inflexible unity of Church and State was fifteenth-century Spain where Catholicism was official and mandatory. Because it was against the law to practice any other religion (that is, it was a criminal act), the sizable Jewish population had either to convert, flee, or be executed.

Nothing of the sort was to be tolerated in the United States, and it never has. But still, over the years, it has been traditional to open official government functions and sessions — even the United States Senate — with prayers; and our coins bear the motto "In God we trust." Generation after generation of school children listened to Bible readings and said prayers in public schools. It began to occur to some people that the "wall of separation between Church and State" was full of holes.

Some of the holes that have created strife in recent years are the use of public funds to purchase books for parochial schools, or to transport children by bus to and from those schools; the release of children from public school so that they can attend religious classes elsewhere; and Bible reading or recitation of prayers in public schools.

In 1951, the New York State Board of Regents thought it was time to put an end to the argument about religion in its own schools, but in an effort to do so, the regents unintentionally laid the groundwork for a battle which raged until the Supreme Court brought it to an end with a major decision.

It all began with what seemed like a simple prayer. For a long time, a number of non-Christian parents had objected to the use of the Christian Lord's Prayer in public schools. The regents' solution to the problem was to offer the schools an original prayer that was nonsectarian. It read: *"Almighty God, we acknowledge our dependence upon Thee, and we beg Thy blessings upon us, our parents, our teachers, and our Country."* The regents suggested that all New York schools use the prayer, although they were not *required* to.

One of the school boards that did adopt the prayer was in New Hyde Park, a suburban community on Long Island. In 1958, parents were notified that children would be expected to say the prayer in all classrooms each morning. To the board's surprise, the parents of ten of the children protested. They felt that religious training of *any* kind, whether Christian or nonsectarian, was up to parents, not schools. They complained to the school, and when the school authorities turned a deaf ear, the parents went to court.

After a series of defeats in the New York courts, the determined parents finally reached the Supreme Court in 1962. The historic case is known as *Engel* v. *Vitale* (Stephen Engel was one of the parents; William J. Vitale, Jr., a member of the school board; the v. stands for *versus* in this standard form for titling court cases).

In the first decision ever made on school prayers, the Supreme Court ruled that the use of the regents' prayer in the schools was unconstitutional. Justice Black, delivering the Court's opinion said that the *establishment* clause of the First Amendment meant "that in this country it is no part of the business of government to compose official prayers for any group of the American people to recite as part of a religious program carried on by government."

Two more *establishment* clause decisions, which further strengthened the "wall of separation," came in 1963. They were *Abington School District* v. *Schempp* and *Murray* v. *Curlett*.

During the 1956-57 school year, Ellory Schempp was a junior in a school in Abington Township, Pennsylvania. He was a Unitarian with strong feelings about freedom of religious belief. According to Pennsylvania law at that time, all school pupils were expected to listen to a daily reading of ten verses from the King James version of the Bible and then recite the Lord's Prayer.

Ellory Schempp asked to be excused from such religious exercises in school since to participate went against his creed; he was told that it was impossible to be excused. His angry parents, with help from the Legal Aid Society, brought suit against the local board for violating the establishment clause of the First Amendment.

A Federal District Court in Pennsylvania ruled that both the Bible reading and the recitation of the Lord's Prayer were unconstitutional; the use of the New Testament prayer showed a preference for the Christian religion, and reading from the Bible without comment was offensive to Unitarians who do not interpret the Bible literally.

Determined to restore religion to their schools, the school board appealed the case and took it to the Surpreme Court. As a result, both Bible reading and the use of the Lord's Prayer were barred from all public schools across the nation.

It is curious to note that few decisions have caused such widespread outrage and defiance in America — the country founded for religious freedom. According to figures printed in *The Philadelphia Bulletin* in late 1970, half the school districts in the South and nearly a fifth of those in the state of Pennsylvania were still using the Bible or the Lord's Prayer in their schools in direct violation of the Court ruling. There are other areas of the country, too, where popular feeling about the importance of prayer in public schools is very strong. If this ever becomes a *prevailing* opinion throughout the country, it is possible that the law will have to be changed again.

During the time that the Schempp case was making its way through the courts, William J. Murray III was an eighth-grader in Baltimore, Maryland. The schools of that city began each day with a Bible reading and/or the Lord's Prayer. William Murray and his mother, Madalyn, were atheists. William asked to be excused from the classroom while the religious observances were taking place, but he, too, was refused permission.

Mrs. Murray was distressed enough to keep her son home from school for the next two weeks. She then decided that it would make more sense to fight the legality of religious exercises in schools once and for all, and so she brought suit in a Maryland court. In due time, the case reached the Supreme Court, simultaneously, as it happened, with the Schempp case, and the two were decided together.

Justice Tom C. Clark read the opinion of the Court. After discussing the *establishment* clause and the need for separation of Church and State, he went on:

> The place of religion in our society is an exalted
> one, achieved through a long tradition of reliance
> on the home, the Church, and the inviolable citadel
> of the individual heart and mind. We have come
> to recognize through bitter experience that it is
> not within the power of government to invade that
> citadel, whether its purpose or effects be to aid or
> oppose, to advance or retard. In the relationship
> between man and religion, the State is firmly com-
> mitted to a position of neutrality.

The Murrays won their case and a victory for the Bill of Rights — but it was no longer possible for them to live in Baltimore. Mrs. Murray was fired from her job, the windows of her house were smashed, her garden uprooted, the Murray children were beaten and pelted with rotten eggs; the family car had its tires slashed, and once, someone shot at it with a gun. The Murrays gave up and moved to Hawaii.

A school case that involved the *free exercise* clause of the First Amendment got that issue off to a poor start in 1940 with *Minersville School District* v. *Gobitis.* Children who were members of the Jehovah's Witness sect wanted to be excused from saluting the flag because pledges of allegiance violated their religious beliefs. The Supreme Court upheld the school board, and the children were forced to take part in the flag-salute exercises whether they liked it or not.

But within two years, three of the Justices who agreed with the Court's decision had all changed their minds. In their dissenting opinion in another case in 1942 *(Jones* v. *Opelika)* they wrote jointly: *"Since we joined in the opinion in the Gobitis case, we think this is an appropriate occasion to state that we now believe that it was also wrongly decided."*

The following year, 1943, gave the three the chance to correct their mistake. They were helped by the fact that the Supreme Court now also had two new Justices, Jackson and Rutledge, who agreed with them, and they all joined in outlawing the compulsory flag salute in schools in *West Virginia State Board of Education* v. *Barnette.*

The case came about when seven children of the Jehovah's Witness Barnette family objected to saluting the flag in school each day as required by West Virginia law. The seven children were expelled from school.

Walter Barnette fought the case all the way to the Supreme Court, and he won it. Justice Robert H. Jackson, delivering the Court's opinion on this occasion said:

Freedom to differ is not limited to things that do not matter much. That would be a mere shadow of freedom. The test of its substance is the right to differ as to things that touch the heart of the existing order.

If there is any fixed star in our constitutional constellation, it is that no official, high or petty, can prescribe what shall be orthodox in politics, nationalism, religion, or other matters of opinion or force citizens to confess by word or act of faith, their faith therein.

Even though this was a case based originally on free exercise of religion, Justice Jackson said while speaking for the Court, "The flag salute is a form of utterance." Because the discussion involved the *free speech* clause, and freedom of speech also means freedom *not* to speak, no one can now be required to salute the flag, no matter *what* his reason. The decision came on Flag Day, June 14, 1943.

Justice Black referred to this historic change of opinion twenty-five years later when discussing *Gobitis* in his book, *A Constitutional Faith:*

Long reflection convinced me that although the principle was sound, its application in the particular case was wrong, and I clearly stated this change of view in a concurring opinion in *Barnette* which Justice Douglas joined. Life itself is change and one who fails to recognize this must indeed be narrow-minded. . . .

Religious freedom has not been tested only in schools. Such diverse matters as Sunday closing of stores, taxes on sales of religious books, and the practice of polygamy — marriage to more than one person at a time — have come up for debate. One of the issues that figured very largely in the upheavals of the 1960's was the question of military draft exemption.

The *1965 Draft Act Cases* involved three men, Daniel A. Seeger, Arno S. Jakobson, and Forest B. Peter. All three had refused to be inducted into the Army because they were conscientious objectors. Historically, such objection had been based *only* on religious belief. The World War I draft statutes exempted members of "peace churches" or "a pacifist religious sect." By 1940, the draft rules no longer required membership, but exempted those whose opposition to war was based on "religious training and belief." In 1951, Congress defined this as follows:

> Religious training and belief in this connection means an individual belief in a relation to a Supreme Being involving duties superior to those arising from any human relation, but does not include essentially political, sociological or philosophical views, or a merely personal moral code.

In 1965, Seeger stated that he was opposed to participation to war in any form, but he would not say whether or not he believed in a Supreme Being. Jakobson claimed belief in a Supreme Being who was "Creator of Man," who was "ultimately responsible for the existence of" man. Peter's belief was in "our democratic American culture, with its values derived from the Western religious and philosophical tradition." Peter continued that he supposed "you could call that a belief in the Supreme Being or God. These just do not happen to be the words I use."

In its decision, *United States* v. *Seeger,* the Supreme Court ruled that the three men were entitled to exemption as conscientious objectors because the beliefs they held were sincere and meaningful and occupied the same place in their lives as belief in God would. This marked the first time that sincere beliefs of a non-religious nature were held to be as meaningful as those directly involving God.

While there was far less reaction from the public at large than there had been in the school prayer and flag-salute cases, both Congress and the Johnson Administration expressed dissatisfaction with the *Seeger* decision. Congress, led by a furious Congressman Rivers, chairman of the House Armed Services Committee, immediately amended the draft law so that it read very much like the old provision of 1951. Those responsible for drafting men to fight in the Vietnam War did not want to make it easy for dissenters (of which there were many) to escape. The law was made to read: *"Religious training and belief does not include essentially political, sociological or philosophical views, or a merely personal code."*

The difference from the old law was the omission of the term "Supreme Being," which now made the *Seeger* decision meaningless. But fortunately, the provision had a short life. It was ruled unconstitutional in 1969.

Religion and the draft law had to be tested yet again, and the opportunity came the following year, 1970, when *Welsh* v. *United States* reached the Supreme Court. Elliot A. Welsh, II, a twenty-eight-year-old professional man from Los Angeles, had asked for exemption from the military service in 1964 on the grounds of conscientious objection. When he filled in the application form, he carefully crossed out the words "religious training." Showing no religious beliefs of any kind, Welsh's application was denied, and he was sentenced to jail for three years when he refused to be inducted into the Army. Mr. Welsh appealed, his case reached the Supreme Court, and his sentence was reversed. The Court ruled that the law excuses "all those whose consciences, spurred by deeply held moral, ethical or religious beliefs, would give them no rest or peace if they allowed themselves to become a part of an instrument of war."

While Welsh had claimed no religious beliefs of any kind, he had stressed that he believed "the taking of life—anyone's life—to be morally wrong." In accepting that, the Court had gone even further than it had in the *Seeger* decision, which was based on beliefs comparable to a belief in God. At last, the separation between Church and State, in the draft laws at least, was complete.

At another period in history it would have been unthinkable for any man to deny that fighting for one's country—right or wrong—was the honorable thing to do. But by 1970, so many people felt that the taking of life was morally wrong, that the *Welsh* decision was made possible. As a result of it, the very sense of "freedom of religion" was altered, for it came to include the freedom to have no religion at all.

It is impossible to know what the framers of the Constitution would have thought of the interpretations of the First Amendment recounted in this chapter—but they could only have been deeply pleased with the flexibility of the document they had created, with its ability to change with the times.

Senator Joseph McCarthy in action

The
Right
to Speak

Congress shall make no law . . . abridging the freedom of speech, or of the press . . .

AMENDMENT I

WHEN THE BILL OF RIGHTS was written, *speech* meant face-to-face conversation and *the press* meant newspapers, magazines, and books.

Today, in addition to a morass of printed matter, we have radio, television, films, and photographs, and so, through the flexibility of the Constitution, freedom of speech and of the press has come to mean freedom of *expression*. As we shall see, it has even been interpreted to mean freedom of *action* when some form of non-verbal behavior was used to communicate an idea.

The right to free expression is basic to America.

Mr. Justice Black expressed it eloquently in 1941 when he wrote (*Milk Wagon Drivers Union* v. *Meadowmoor Dairies*):

> Freedom to speak and write about public questions is as important to the life of our government as is the heart of the human body. In fact, this privilege is the heart of our government! If that heart be weakened, the result is debilitation; if it be stilled, the result is death.

The sentiment expressed by Justice Black is so obviously true, it hardly seems possible that anyone could argue with it. Yet, not only have there been many who could, but many who have — and once in a while, with reason. For under special circumstances, it is sometimes necessary to curb speech. The doctrine used to determine the appropriate circumstances has come to be known as the "clear and present danger" test.

The case that led to the use of that term began in 1917, during World War I, when Charles T. Schenck, general secretary of the Socialist Party, together with some of his fellow members, sent out fifteen thousand leaflets to young men urging them to resist conscription into military service.

Schenck and his friends were arrested and indicted under the Espionage Act, which had been passed that same year. Accused of conspiracy to cause insubordination in the armed forces, obstructing the draft, and unlawfully using the mails, the men were tried and convicted. They appealed on the grounds that their right to free speech had been violated, and the case, *Schenck* v. *United States*, reached the Supreme Court in 1919.

The Court was unanimous in upholding the prisoners' conviction. In explaining the Court's opinion, Justice Oliver Wendell Holmes, Jr., then seventy-eight years old, used an example that has become classic. He said that in ordinary times (peacetime), the defendants would have been free, within the Constitution, to write their pamphlets; however, the circumstances, as well as the act, must always be considered. The right to free speech would not protect a man who falsely shouted "Fire" in a theater and caused a panic. Such an act would create a *clear and present danger,* and so must be prevented.

Mr. Justice Holmes was saying that the rights of an individual can*not* be protected when they are clearly dangerous to society or to the nation. Some things that are safely said in normal times become dangerous in time of war.

The *clear and present danger* test has been used many times over in deciding questions of free expression. For a while, other, less liberal, tests were used, but by the late 1950's, the *clear and present danger* test was once more in use by the Court and has remained so.

One of the worst — if not *the* worst — periods for free expression in America came on the heels of World War II. The Smith Act (1940), the McCarran Act (1950), and the Communist Control Act (1954) were all designed to protect the government against possible destruction by violence or alliance with a foreign government.

With the same motive, President Truman, in 1947, had set up a Federal loyalty program to ferret out disloyal and subversive elements in government employ. Riding on the coattails of that program, and in the atmosphere of anxiety caused by the Korean War and the Cold War with the Soviet Union, Senator Joseph McCarthy rose to prominence. His Un-American Activities Committee (better known as the McCarthy Committee) began a tireless hunt for alleged Communists in government, the Army, and in private life. By December, 1952, no less than 6.6 million people had been investigated by the committee. Although not a single case of espionage was discovered, thousands of people lost their jobs.

After President Eisenhower was inaugurated in 1953, McCarthy threw off any restraint he may have

felt before. He unleashed attacks on the State
Department and the Voice of America. Many
foreign service personnel, with records of excellent
service, were summarily fired as a result. State
Department libraries were ordered to remove from
their shelves all books by authors who were "tainted"
by Communist leanings; the works of Tom Paine
were among those banned, and many books were
actually burned.

A network of so-called national security measures
sprang up around the country, and people everywhere were harassed and persecuted by such means
as blacklists, secret informers, intimidation, guilt
by association — all methods that Americans have
traditionally thought of as subversive and foreign
to the United States.

Judge Learned Hand expressed the feelings of
many Americans when he said:

> I believe that that community is already in process
> of dissolution where each man begins to eye his
> neighbor as a possible enemy, where noncon-
> formity with the accepted creed, political as well
> as religious, is a mark of disaffection; where de-
> nunciation, without specification or backing, takes
> the place of evidence.

McCarthy finally went too far when he attacked
the U.S. Army. The Army fought back, and the

heated hearings that took place as a result were finally televised for the public to see and hear. From April 22 to June 17, 1954, an astounded audience of as many as twenty million Americans witnessed the rantings and the unsupported accusations of McCarthy.

It is to America's credit that when the nation saw the real extent of McCarthy's activities, it was literally shocked into its senses. There was an outcry across the land that reached right into Congress; McCarthy was censured by the U.S. Senate in a sixty-seven to twenty-two vote and his investigations were stopped. In 1957, he died, mourned by relatively few.

After this unfortunate period, we returned to a belief in free speech, and the Supreme Court ruled that speaking in favor of Communism was *not* the same as an act against the government. It even became legal to belong to the Communist Party — and then it appeared that very few people did.

There were free-expression cases of all kinds during the 1960's; some of them clarified in more detail decisions that had been made in recent years, but some of them were quite different from any that had gone before.

One of these began when Mary Beth Tinker, a thirteen-year-old junior high school student in Des

Moines, Iowa, came to school wearing a black armband. If someone in her family had died, Mary Beth would have received everyone's sympathy — but that was not the case. She wore the armband, she said, to mourn her country's questionable participation in the Vietnam War. Not only did Mary Beth's teachers lack sympathy, they sent her home from school.

Mr. and Mrs. Tinker thought the school had behaved improperly, and they took the matter to court. Four years later they reached the Supreme Court, and Mary Beth Tinker won a victory. So did students everywhere, for in ruling on *Tinker* v. *Des Moines School District, et al.*, the Court decided that wearing an armband was a form of symbolic speech and, "It can hardly be argued that either students or teachers shed their constitutional rights to freedom of speech or expression at the schoolhouse gate."

In sharp disagreement with the Court, Justice Hugo Black wrote a stinging dissent in which he said that after such a ruling, students "will be ready, able and willing to defy their teachers on practically all orders. This is the more unfortunate for the schools since groups of students all over the land are already running loose, conducting break-ins, sit-ins, lie-ins, and smash-ins."

Long hair came up for discussion in the courts, too, by courtesy of two high school students who were expelled from their school in Williams Bay, Wisconsin. Over the 1968 summer vacation, the boys had let their hair grow long, and when they returned to school in September they were found to be in violation of a school rule that read (in violation itself — of the rules of grammar!):

> Hair should be washed, combed and worn so it does not hang below the collar line in the back, over the ears on the side and must be above the eyebrows. Boys should be clean shaven long sideburns are out.

The parents of the boys took the matter of the expulsion to court, and in the Seventh Circuit Court of Appeals they won their point and a right for all students. The court ruled that there were no laws to dictate the length of adults' hair, and students were entitled to the hair length they chose as a form of free expression under the First Amendment. In 1970, the Supreme Court, apparently believing that it could make no further contribution, refused to review the case, and so the decision has remained.

While wearing long hair was, happily, defined as a form of free expression, another kind of behavior did not fare as well. In 1966, David P. O'Brien burned his draft card in front of a Boston courthouse. He was immediately arrested by FBI agents and convicted under a law which required that draft cards be carried at all times.

O'Brien appealed the conviction on the grounds that burning the card was a form of symbolic speech and as such, was protected under the First Amendment. The Supreme Court disagreed. In delivering the opinion, Chief Justice Warren said, "We cannot accept the view that an apparently limitless variety of conduct can be labeled 'speech.'"

It seems thoroughly inconsistent to apply the term "speech" to the wearing of an armband, but not to the burning of a draft card. However, it can certainly be argued that armband-wearing does not in any way interfere with the administration of our laws, while burning a draft card does. For those who were opposed to draft cards in the first place, this argument is a poor one, and the entire issue becomes difficult to resolve. Freedom of expression is often a difficult area in which to draw sharp boundaries, and our courts have long had to struggle with it.

During the same period that so many *speech* decisions were made, there were a number of trials for freedom of the press, too, and in most of them freedom won. Actually, with the extension of the meaning of *free speech* to *free expression*, the problems of a free press are not as unique as they used to be. *Speech* and *press* tend to overlap and blend, although some different terms may be used.

When a newspaper is told by the government what it may print, or when a book may not be sold, we refer to the interference as censorship. Censorship and the written word have been in conflict ever since the Constitution was framed, because, although freedom of the press is guaranteed, the government may legally interfere if the material is dangerous to public safety or welfare. The delicate problem has been to protect the freedom of ideas which ought to be protected under the First Amendment while censoring the dangerous ones before they are published. The *clear and present danger* test has to be used once more.

The problem is that once the material has been published and distributed, it is too late to censor it; the damage has been done. On the other hand, if the ideas have not yet been expressed, who can say whether they would be dangerous or not? Clearly, it is a thin line to walk and one which has given the Supreme Court trouble for years. The trouble has lessened somewhat as our concept of what is "dangerous" has changed and sharply narrowed.

A constant problem area lies between the right of a free press to report the news together with comment that adds to public understanding of current events, and the right of a court to ensure a fair trial. People find out what is happening in the world chiefly through the printed word, or through radio and television, and they have a right to know as much as possible. But how unbiased can any trial be when the media have covered the story in such a way that prospective jurors may have virtually made up their minds about the guilt or innocence of the accused before he ever enters a courtroom?

In more than one case, the Supreme Court has reversed murder convictions because the jury had been influenced by the press or because television cameras in the courtroom created a carnival atmosphere. Dr. Samuel Sheppard, accused and convicted of murdering his wife, had the conviction overturned (and was ultimately freed) by the Supreme Court in 1966 because of what Mr. Justice Clark referred to as a circus atmosphere during the trial. Clark repeated the same concern the Court had expressed a year before in reversing the conviction of Billie Sol Estes, accused of swindling, that the presence of many reporters can deny the accused the "judicial serenity and calm" necessary for a fair trial, even if it cannot be shown that the jury was influenced by the publicity. In reporting on the Estes trial, *The New York Times* said, "The courtroom was turned into a snake-pit by the multiplicity of cameras, wires, microphones and technicians milling about the chamber." Permitting full reportage of a controversial case while retaining the dignity of the courtroom poses a dilemma which has yet to be solved.

Some other kinds of *free speech* situations are much simpler. When *The New York Times* began publication of the Pentagon Papers, a series of classified documents obtained from Daniel Ellsberg and dealing with United States involvement in Southeast Asia (a matter embarassing to the Nixon Administration), the government tried to stop the paper from publishing the series. In *The New York Times* v. *United States*, 1971, the Court found by a 6 to 3 majority that the government had failed to prove that publication constituted "immediate and irreparable harm to the nation." The Papers were printed.

A totally different area of free expression — and surely the one that most captured the imagination and interest of the public — is that centering around obscenity. It is hard to say just what obscenity is. According to the dictionary it means:

1. that which is offensive to modesty or decency;
   lewd.
2. that which causes, or is intended to cause,
   sexual excitement or lust.

Unfortunately, the dictionary is unable to tell us
whose sense of modesty or decency might be
offended, or in *whom* it might cause lust. We have
all met people who seem *never* to be offended. But
then, what is perfectly normal, realistic, or in-
structive to some citizens, may be considered obscene by others. Chief Justice Warren declared
obscenity to be the Court's "most difficult" area to
define.

The law, now much relaxed about many books
and films that were formerly considered obscene,
still has regulations regarding "hard-core (obvious
or blatant) pornography." On one occasion, Justice
Stewart said that he favored censorship *only* if
the material represented hard-core pornography,
but when asked for a definition of the term, all that
the Justice could say is, "I know it when I see it."
Justice Harlan offered as *his* definition, "That
prurient material that is patently offensive or whose
indecency is self-demonstrating." Other definitions
of obscenity have been similarly vague, most of
them relying on words that need definition in them-

selves: vile, lewd, filthy, lascivious, and so forth.

During the decade of the sixties, there was a notable loosening of standards of morality and ideas of decency. Sex began to be accepted as a normal and natural function, and frank discussion of it by "nice" people, in schools, in print, and in films became the norm. Puritan purity was on the way out. The change in mores had to affect our laws.

A first hint of things to come was the publication in this country of the D. H. Lawrence novel, *Lady Chatterley's Lover*, in 1959. Containing detailed descriptions of sexual acts, the book had been officially banned here since 1928, although "bootlegged" copies of foreign editions were widely circulated.

In 1966, the Supreme Court finally lifted a ban on the sale of *John Cleland's Memoirs of a Woman of Pleasure*, more popularly known as *Fanny Hill*, in the state of Massachusetts. The book had originally appeared in print in England in 1749.

But by contrast, it was also in 1966 that Ralph Ginzburg was fined $28,000 and sentenced to five years in prison for publishing and mailing an "obscene" magazine and other literature. The Supreme Court upheld Mr. Ginzburg's conviction by the slim majority of 5 to 4, not so much because of the content of the publications themselves, but rather because of the advertising and promotion they received and which the Court found filled with "the leer of the sensualist."

So difficult was this decision, that all four of the dissenting Justices — Black, Douglas, Stewart, and Harlan — wrote separate opinions. Shortly after *Ginzburg* v. *United States*, however, the Justices seemed to be more in accord on the elimination of censorship, and most of the decisions that followed worked to this end. By the last years of the decade, audiences were jamming theaters to see the Swedish movie *I Am Curious (Yellow)*, with its many explicit sex scenes, and the musical show *Hair* in which nude actors and actresses appeared on the legitimate stage.

As these developments began to take place, most people were concerned that children and teen-agers might not be able to deal in a comfortable way with pornographic material and should be protected from it. To this end, the movie industry instituted a rating system for films which prohibits minors from attending some, and admits them to some others when accompanied by an adult. There are also laws and regulations to prevent the sale of pornographic books to young people.

In spite of these few restraints, the over-all

letting down of barriers was so great that it gave
rise to an "epidemic" of public nudity and per-
formances with high sexual content; as a result,
some restrictive action was begun all over again.
The backlash started when the movie *Deep Throat*
was banned in New York City in 1973, and the
theater that had exhibited it was fined a large sum
of money.

In a much more serious, and rather alarming
action, the Supreme Court, in June, 1973, handed
down a new set of rulings on obscenity. Arguing
that tastes and sensibilities vary in different communities, the Court, in a 5 to 4 decision, ruled
that individual states may ban books, magazines,
plays, or films if they are offensive to local standards. Chief Justice Burger wrote the majority
opinion.

Most people would agree that the public should
be protected from offensive displays that cannot
be avoided by those who do not wish to view
them — displays on signs, or in shop windows, for
example. But clearly, anyone who does not want
to see a pornographic film is free to stay away, and
no one is ever forced to buy or read a pornographic
book; on the other hand, because obscenity is so
hard to define, works of quality and lasting value
may be banned along with the worthless, and many

people feel that the individual should be free to decide for himself. To permit the establishment of local censors to dictate which books or films may be offered to the public is a direct attack on the First Amendment and a step backward for all of us.

Marchers listening to "I have a dream . . ."

We
Gather
Together

Congress shall make no law . . . abridging . . . the right of the people peaceably to assemble, and to petition the Government for a redress of grievances.

AMENDMENT I

IT WAS NOT until 1689 that British subjects had the right to *petition for redress of grievances* — to ask the government to remedy the complaints they had about administrative matters. But even though the right existed by the time the Colonists came to the New World, and even though they were still British subjects, they discovered that by leaving England they had lost the right to petition along with many other privileges. They carefully made the point in the Declaration of Independence that even though they had asked for redress, they were "answered only by repeated injury."

Under no circumstances did they want to have the same problems in the United States, and so the right to petition was written into the Bill of Rights. And because citizens had to meet if they were to discuss the grievances they thought should be corrected, they included the right to *assembly*, to hold meetings, too.

Americans take for granted the right to get together for meetings of all sorts, for parties, parades, or for cultural or sports events, but in many times and places, people were forbidden to gather together. Undemocratic governments have always known that as long as they could keep people from assembling, they could keep them under control. No people can rebel or overthrow a government if each individual has to act alone.

As we have seen before, restrictions are sometimes necessary for the sake of public safety, even though they may interfere with individual rights. The clear and present danger test applies to *assembly* as well as to *expression*. When large public gatherings are held, it is reasonable to control them in such a way that riots, stampedes, or panic are avoided. It is also necessary to permit the flow of traffic, particularly where emergency vehicles such as ambulances or fire engines might have to travel. It is always important to protect human life and safety—but the line between preventing real danger and interfering with freedom may be a hard one to draw. This distinction is subject both to honest confusion and to downright abuse.

A city may reasonably require a permit for a parade or demonstration in order to manage traffic safely, but the withholding of a permit becomes highly improper if it is done mainly to control the right to freedom of assembly or speech. In Jersey City, the misuse of one such permit regulation resulted in the Supreme Court's decision (*Hague* v. *CIO*, 1939) declaring the city's entire permit law invalid.

The CIO had applied for permission to hold a union meeting. According to the ordinance, permits could be refused in order to prevent riots, disturbances, or disorderly activity. But the CIO was refused *its* request because the director of public safety thought that the union members were Communists and the aims of the organization "communistic." The Court made it plain that permits for public meetings could be refused when safety was endangered, but *not* because of the director's political opinions.

There have been many efforts to halt union activities in this fashion, and in the majority of cases the Supreme Court has protected the right to peaceful assembly. There have been a large number of cases involving picketing and, sometimes, these have been difficult to decide. In one case, *Thornhill* v. *Alabama*, 1940, the Court ruled that there could be no law that prohibited picketing; on other occasions, the Court has ruled against picketing if there was a possibility of violence or when picketing was used to exert economic pressure. In the main, the policy has been that peaceful picketing is a way of telling the public what is happening, and it is protected by the First Amendment.

Local ordinances governing meetings have frequently been used against unpopular assemblies other than union meetings. Some of these are ethnic groups, students, and political organizations.

In 1937, a man named Dirk De Jonge spoke at a meeting of the Communist Party in Portland, Oregon. The meeting had been called to protest alleged brutality on the part of the Portland police.

Although the meeting was a peaceful one, De Jonge was arrested and indicted under the local law that made it a criminal offense to advocate "crime, physical violence, sabotage, or any unlawful acts or methods as a means of accomplishing industrial change or political revolution." De Jonge wasn't guilty of any of those things and, in fact, wasn't even charged with them directly. The court was *assuming* that the Communist Party was in violation of the statute, and De Jonge was guilty because he was a member of the party. He was sentenced to seven years in prison.

De Jonge's lawyer pointed out that De Jonge had addressed a meeting that was not called to advocate crime, but to ask for a redress of grievances — the alleged police brutality. De Jonge himself spoke not of violence, but rather, discussed a maritime union strike.

The Supreme Court decided unanimously in De Jonge's favor (*De Jonge* v. *Oregon*). In reading the opinion, Chief Justice Hughes noted that "peaceable assembly for lawful discussion, however unpopular the sponsorship, cannot be made a crime." And, "The holding of meetings for peaceful political action cannot be proscribed. Those who assist in the conduct of such meetings cannot be branded as criminals on that score." The right to freedom of peaceful assembly was upheld.

In another kind of situation, the Court reached a different kind of conclusion. During the late 1940's, a youth named Irving Feiner attracted a crowd of black and white listeners as he made a sidewalk speech in Syracuse, New York. He was angry because an organization called the Young Progressives had just had to hire a hotel hall for its meeting,

planned for that evening, because a permit to use
the school had suddenly been revoked. In his tirade,
Feiner referred to both President Truman and New
York City's Mayor O'Dwyer as "bums." He called
Mayor Costello of Syracuse a "champagne-sipping
bum." After getting more and more abusive and
irate, he yelled, "The Negroes don't have equal
rights; they should rise up in arms and fight for
them."

One or another of Feiner's remarks angered
different members of the crowd and they began to
mutter and grumble among themselves. Finally
someone shouted that if the police would not remove Feiner from the stand, he would do it himself. The crowd murmured approval and inched in
just a little closer.

The police sensed the threat and feared that
serious trouble was about to erupt. They twice asked
Feiner to stop talking, and when he went right on,
the policemen arrested him.

Feiner protested his arrest in court, but in this
case, the State Court of Appeals found the policemen were justified in making the arrest. The judge
felt that Feiner, "with intent to provoke a breach
of the peace and with knowledge of the conse-
quences, so inflamed and agitated a mixed audience
of sympathizers and opponents that, in the judg-

ment of the police officers present, a clear and present danger of disorder and violence was threatened."

The Supreme Court, in *Feiner* v. *New York*, 1951, agreed with the lower courts. Chief Justice Vinson made it plain that there was no question about Feiner's right to hold the meeting or to make derogatory remarks about public officials, but that the police were justified in arresting him because they

> were motivated solely by a proper concern for the preservation of order and protection of the general welfare, and that there was no evidence which could lend color to a claim that the acts of the police were a cover for suppression of [Feiner's] views and opinions. Petitioner was thus neither arrested nor convicted for the making or the content of his speech. Rather, it was the reaction which it actually engendered.

Here, the public safety was really in jeopardy and the clear and present danger test was brought into play.

As the United States entered the 1960's, there were unprecedented numbers of tests of the right to assembly. There were sit-ins, ride-ins, sleep-ins, teach-ins, and more marches and demonstrations than anyone could count. They protested the highly unpopular Vietnam War, pollution, the military draft, racial discrimination, poor housing, and "Establishment values"; they made demands for peace, aid to poor people, student power, legalized abortion, equality for ethnic groups, women, and homosexuals, and for other rights as well.

In California, rallying behind leader César Chávez of the United Farm Workers, migratory workers fought for—and eventually won—better wages and conditions. American Indians, long the poorest of our citizens, became more militant and began to demand better treatment. Chicanos, Italian-Americans, and Puerto Ricans (who, in 1970, succeeded in electing Herman Badillo, the first Puerto Rican congressman) all made their bids for recognition.

Reactionary, neo-Nazi, and other right-wing groups proliferated, too, and exercised their legal right to peaceable assembly in protest against the advances that were taking place in more liberal spheres.

Student demonstrations, perhaps more than any other, have taxed our legislators on the questions of freedom of assembly and speech. The sight of students carrying guns or looting campus offices shocked the nation, but the sight of troops pointing rifles—and actually shooting them—was even more shocking. While the right to assemble and to petition is unarguable, it is clear that all of us, young and old alike, can still be confused in our ability to exercise it safely.

With the end of the Vietnam War and the draft, campuses seem to have settled down. At the present time, at least, there appears to be an end to violence and a return to more intellectual forms of protest. As for those years of upheaval and anger that have just passed, it is possible that in spite of the lives that were lost, the young rebels who dared to declare themselves independent from England for the sake of their rights would have been sympathetic.

*James McCord showing telephone with
bug at Watergate hearing, 1973*

The
Right
to Privacy

The right of the people to be secure in their persons, houses, papers, and effects . . . shall not be violated . . .
AMENDMENT IV

THERE WAS A TIME when law-enforcement officers trying to solve a crime had the right to stop passersby on the street and search them. They could also enter anyone's home, at any hour, and look through drawers, closets, basement, or attic in the hope that they would discover the secret papers, the murder weapon, illegal drugs, or the missing body. Sometimes they found whatever it was they were looking for, but most of the time, innocent people were inconvenienced, or worse, embarrassed, harassed, and humiliated.

Such "fishing expeditions" are the stuff of which thriller films are made; an ominous pounding at the door in the middle of the night chills the bones of all. Often the police are so threatening, the mere fact of their presence so menacing, that the innocent tremble as well as the guilty. Melodrama like this may be fine in films, but clearly, there is no place for it in a democracy. We all have the right to feel safe, secure, and private in our homes and in our lives, with the knowledge that no one can — legally — break in upon us unexpectedly. It was just for this reason that the Fourth Amendment was added to the Constitution.

Since we aren't always at home, the Fourth applies not only to houses but to such places as business offices, cars, hotel rooms, and — far-fetched though it sounds — even to telephone booths.

Telephones have brought a new dimension to our right to privacy: if someone taps your telephone line and listens to your conversation, is he violating the Fourth Amendment? He is not physically in your house, or searching your person or your papers, but he is most certainly invading your privacy. Even if you are not engaged in crime, how many of your telephone conversations would you care to have overheard by a stranger or recorded on tape to be played for an audience? No one likes the idea, and yet, wiretapping and other kinds of electronic surveillance have become sufficiently widespread to create a serious problem for the lawmakers.

In 1967, the Supreme Court overturned the conviction of Charles Katz (*Katz* v. *United States*), a
gambler who regularly made phone calls from the
same booth on Hollywood's Sunset Boulevard. The
FBI tapped the phone and Katz was convicted on
the evidence gathered.

The Court ruled that the FBI had, in effect,
"seized" Katz's conversation just as if it had been
a piece of property, and therefore had violated his
Constitutional rights since the seizure was made
without a warrant. In this case, as in many others,
there was good reason to believe that the defendant
was a law-breaker, but he was a citizen first, and his
Constitutional rights were protected nonetheless.

In most cases, the law requires that searches and
seizures be made only with a warrant—a legal
document that permits such action. To get a warrant,
you have to describe the crime you believe was
committed, and you must describe the person or
place to be searched or seized so as to avoid error.
In other words, you can't simply walk into the police
station and ask for a warrant to have your neighbor
arrested or to have his car searched. You must have
an excellent reason to think he is breaking the law
and you must be sure of your facts. In the phrases
of the Constitution, persons are protected against
"unreasonable searches and seizures," and "no
Warrants shall issue, but upon probable cause. . ."

It is easy to imagine the confusion that has surrounded the terms "unreasonable" and "probable cause."

It *is* considered "reasonable" (and therefore legal) for a policeman to make an arrest without a warrant when he actually *sees* a crime being committed; he may also search or make an arrest when he has good reason to *believe* that a felony (serious crime) was committed. If, for instance, he hears a shot, sees a dead body, and a man fleeing with a smoking gun in his hand, he has good reason to arrest the man with the gun. Unfortunately, the situation is rarely so clearcut and mistakes are often made. In the same situation, if the officer does *not* see a gunman, but he *does* see, lurking in a dark doorway, a couple of teenagers who have already had some minor trouble with the law, he might be very much tempted to arrest them, or at least to search them for weapons. But would the policeman's "good reason" be good enough to satisfy the law? In most cases, no.

Especially since the increase in crime that came with the general unrest of the sixties and the resulting concern for law and order that accompanied it, Americans are often both unlawfully and unjustly arrested and/or searched.

In some localities, it is almost routine to search the cars of young people, on one pretext or another, to look for marijuana. Such searches are illegal, but unfortunately, the victims rarely know the law.

A case in which citizens themselves were called upon to make decisions is the result of the "epidemic" of airplane hijackings of the early 1970's. As a security measure, airlines were forced to search all passengers boarding planes to make sure they carried no weapons. There was no illegality here since passengers were free to refuse to be searched; the airline, however, was free to keep them from boarding the plane—and if the passengers really wanted to go on the flight, they had to solve the problem by agreeing to the search.

Such decisions are not usually up to the citizens involved, but then the problem shifts to those who do have to decide. In the problem area of wiretapping, the rulings have undergone a series of changes shifting it from illegal to legal in various circumstances. At the present time, the matter is still largely in controversy, but there *are* some situations in which evidence obtained by electronic devices is legal. It is a dangerous law, for while "bugging" has been used with stunning success to round up leaders of organized crime and other law-breakers, it can also be used wrongly to collect evidence of political or other views that are unpopular with society or the government at any given time.

The Watergate scandal of the 1970's is a shocking and dramatic example of the *illegal* use of bugging devices by persons trusted by the entire nation to be above reproach. The revelation in July, 1973, that President Nixon's office and telephones had long been wired to record all conversations — without the knowledge of the persons involved — was dismaying to most Americans. When the facts became public in the course of the Watergate investigation, the President announced that he would discontinue the practice.

Bugging devices themselves are often incredibly ingenious. Not only are microphones hidden in walls, floors, or ceilings, or in such places as fish tanks or flowerpots, but they can be carried in a hearing aid, a watch, or a ring. There is even an ordinary-looking martini olive with a toothpick stuck in it; the "olive" is a tiny transmitter, the "toothpick" its antenna.

Data banks (computers) are another form of technological innovation that have become a source of anxiety about our right to privacy. The Watergate "Plumbers" broke into Dr. Ellsberg's psychiatrist's office to steal his medical records. Had those records been stored in a data bank — as it is projected that all medical records will be one day — the burglary might have been unnecessary; it is likely that those who wanted the records would have had access to the computer center. While there are good medical reasons for having all medical records centrally stored and easily retrievable when needed, it is all too obvious that such a system could be abused.

Similarly, data bank files on criminal records or other matters of a damaging or personal nature are liable to gross misuse. Concerned citizens have begun to protest the use of computerized information about individuals by the government or any government agency. No matter how socially useful such banks may be, the threat to security and privacy seems greater than the benefit.

When citizens are about to be searched by other individuals, not machines, they can sometimes do something to prevent the search if it is unlawful. There is little they can do, however, if they are actually arrested. Not at the moment of arrest, that is. But very shortly thereafter, they can seek the protection of Article I, Section 9, of the Constitution which was designed to keep people from moldering in jail through simple error. The protection is the guarantee of the writ of *habeas corpus*. *Habeas corpus* is Latin for "you shall have the body," and in law, it means just that. If you are improperly arrested or otherwise detained, you have the right to ask a judge or a court to listen to your explanation of the facts and to give you your freedom — your body. If the court agrees that the arrest was improper,

it issues a writ of *habeas corpus* and you are released until your case can be tried. A little-known
fact is that *habeas corpus* does not protect only
persons who have been arrested; it is also available
to those who have been improperly detained any-
where — the Army, a hospital, even a school.

The right to a writ of *habeas corpus* reaches to the
very heart of our democracy. It is one of the things
that makes the dramatic difference between our
kind of government and a totalitarian dictatorship;
there is little possibility in our country that persons
can disappear in the custody of police or other
officers and never be heard from — or of — again.
(It is a fact that in the past it was not uncommon in
the South for illegal treatment of this sort to be
meted out, particularly to blacks, but it is highly
unlikely that such illegal acts could take place
today.) Arrested fairly or not, everyone has a chance
to be heard, although not, unfortunately, as swiftly
as the law would make it appear. Due to enormous
overcrowding of most of our court calendars there
are often long delays before justice is done.

Such unintentional inequities seem to be un-
avoidable at times; so do certain conflicts. We all
want to be protected from dangerous criminals,
but frequently, as in the case of electronic devices,
the searches or arrests of suspicious persons that

are made in an effort to give us that protection, are
at odds with the guaranteed right to privacy. The
problem was much worse in the past than it is now,
for until recently, the Fourth Amendment applied
only to the Federal government and the individual
states were not bound by it. In many states, privacy
was usually the loser when there was a possibility
of apprehending a criminal.

It wasn't until 1961 that a woman named Dollree
Mapp got into some trouble, and, as a result, the
right to freedom from unreasonable search and
seizure to citizens of every state in the Union was
established. Miss Mapp was hardly "heroine"
material; she was, rather, a person of poor reputa-
tion who was suspected of several illegal activities.
(Her case was not unusual. Often, people who by
normal standards are actually inferior citizens
bring about our most important rights legislation.
Justice Felix Frankfurter put it well when he said,
"It is a fair summary of history to say that safeguards
of liberty have been forged in controversies involving not very nice people.") (*United States* v.
Rabinowitz, 1950.)

Dollree Mapp seemed to be one of those "not
very nice people" who was suspected of many in-
fringements of the law. One day, without any notion
that important legal history was about to be made,

some policemen burst into her home to search for betting slips they thought she had. They also seemed to believe that she was hiding a fugitive. As it turned out, the police did not find anything they came to look for, but they *did* find what the trial records called "obscene materials" and "lewd books and pictures." The police seized these items, illegal under Ohio law, and Miss Mapp was tried and convicted for possessing them.

Dollree Mapp's lawyer thought her conviction was unlawful and fought it until the case reached the Supreme Court. The Court agreed that the police had had no right whatsoever to search Miss Mapp's house or take anything that belonged to her, obscene or not. It ruled that the evidence used against her had been illegally obtained and so was worthless as evidence under the Fourth Amendment. Miss Mapp's conviction was reversed; thanks to *Mapp* v. *Ohio*, every American in every state is now protected against unlawful search and seizure in state courts as well as in Federal ones.

The importance of this ruling is illustrated by a pre-Mapp case known as *Rochin* v. *California*, 1952. Antonio Rochin was another person of doubtful character: he was a drug addict who lived in California with his common-law wife.

It was in 1949 that the police received a tip that Rochin was not merely a drug user, but a dealer as well. Three officers rushed off to Rochin's room to look for the "goods." Although they had no search warrant, the men burst in and surprised Rochin, who happened to be sitting on the edge of the bed. The policemen rapidly scanned the room to see what was to be found. One of them noticed two capsules, presumably narcotics, lying on the night-table, and just as he shouted "Whose stuff is this?" Rochin grabbed the capsules and promptly swallowed them.

As the evidence disappeared down Rochin's throat, the frustrated policemen seized Rochin and began to beat him in an effort to make him vomit. When it became clear that they could not — and that the capsules might soon dissolve — they tied up their victim, rushed him to a hospital and had his stomach pumped. The capsules, filled with morphine, duly reappeared and were subsequently presented as evidence at a trial in which Rochin was convicted. He was sentenced to sixty days in jail.

Rochin appealed his conviction but the California District Court of Appeals upheld it. If it had been a Federal court, Rochin could have been freed at once under the Fourth Amendment. But before *Mapp*, the provisions of the Fourth were not binding in California, and so Rochin's conviction remained even though the court found that the officers were "guilty of unlawfully assaulting, battering, torturing

and falsely imprisoning [the] defendant at the
alleged hospital . . ."

After other fruitless efforts at reversal in California, Rochin was finally granted a hearing by the
Supreme Court where his conviction was at last
overturned — *not*, however, on the grounds of violation of the Fourth Amendment, but rather on the due
process clause of the Fourteenth. Making his feelings known in strong language, Justice Frankfurter
declared in reading the decision:

> Illegally breaking into the privacy of the petitioner,
> the struggle to open his mouth and remove what
> was there, the forcible extraction of his stomach's
> contents — this course of proceedings by agents of
> government to obtain evidence is bound to offend
> even hardened sensibilities. They are methods too
> close to the rack and the screw to permit of con-
> stitutional differentiation.

This ideal of protecting the privacy of the individual in his home and in his person is often criticized
on the grounds that it makes the task of law enforce-
ment more difficult.

It is true that it may take longer to track down a
criminal *legally* than it would to illegally stop and
search every suspect in town. And it is even true that
some criminals are never caught at all. But you have
only to imagine how *you* would feel if you knew that
the police could break into your home in the middle

of the day or night in order to search the premises —
or perhaps just to see what you were doing at that
particular time.

It would be unthinkable for Americans to live
under such threat of invasion; the assurance of our
right "to be secure . . . against unreasonable searches
and seizures" is at the very basis of our Constitution
and our liberty. It is one of the essential differences
between a democracy and a totalitarian society.

It is something of a paradox, then, that in order to
protect this fundamental right, the protection must
extend to the criminal as well as to the innocent. But
there is no other way. Without question, a criminal
sometimes benefits by going unpunished for his
crime; it is the price we pay for the freedom to live
in personal privacy and security.

It's what the Bill of Rights was for in the first
place: it meant to protect the citizen against a too-
powerful government that could rob him of his
dignity and freedom. In order for it to work, every
policeman and every official of the state, even of the
very highest levels of our government, must obey the
letter of the law with the same scrupulous care as
any other American. As Mr. Justice Clark aptly com-
mented in *Mapp: "Nothing can destroy a government
more quickly than its failure to observe its own laws,
or worse, its disregard of the charter of its own
existence."*

Young prisoner in a reformatory

The
Rights of
the Accused

No person shall . . . be deprived of life, liberty, or property, without due process of law . . .

AMENDMENT V

THE FIFTH, Sixth, Seventh, and Eighth Amendments all deal with the rights of persons who have been arrested or accused of crimes or who are involved in civil lawsuits. The purpose of such rights is to make certain that no one is treated as if he were guilty unless he is found to be so in a fair trial.

The original Constitution set our nation far in advance of many others of its period by promising the right to a jury trial to those accused of serious crimes. The provision was much expanded by the Fifth Amendment which added assurances that no one could be tried twice for the same crime, nor made to be a witness against himself. (If the jury decides that you did *not* rob the bank, that's it. You're free. The judge can't decide to start the trial over again and keep trying until he gets you convicted. And you don't have to get on the witness stand and say, "Well, yes, I guess I *was* the only person in the bank vault the day it was robbed." You may if you want to, but you don't *have* to.)

The Fifth goes on to say that no one may be deprived of his life, liberty, or property without due process of law. (If they decide to kill you, imprison you, or fine you for that bank robbery, they must do it strictly according to law, allowing you all the rights to which you are entitled.) And, finally, the amendment says that the government may not take anyone's property for government use without paying for it. (If the Pentagon decides to build an airfield right in the middle of your grandfather's farm, they have to pay a fair price for the farm.)

The Sixth Amendment guarantees the right to a speedy and public trial for criminal cases, in the state and district where the act was committed. You cannot be kept in jail for twenty years before the trial, the facts of your trial cannot be kept secret, and you cannot be tried in Nome for a crime you allegedly committed in Charleston. The accused has the right to see anyone who testifies against him; he also has the right to subpoena (to force to appear) witnesses who can testify *for* him. (The judge can't say to you, "Yes, well, uh, we have found you guilty of the bank robbery because this fellow — who doesn't want to be identified — says he saw you do it." If you, on the other hand, were having lunch with someone in Oregon at the time the bank was being robbed in South Carolina, you can legally force your luncheon companion to come to your trial to tell the court where you were — even if he doesn't like you, hates to travel, or simply doesn't want to be bothered.) The accused person is also entitled to the assistance of a lawyer.

The Seventh Amendment has nothing to do with criminal accusations, but it does provide for a jury trial in civil (noncriminal) cases whenever property worth more than twenty dollars is in dispute.

The Eighth Amendment guarantees that excessive bail will not be required, nor excessive fines imposed, and it prohibits cruel and unusual punishments.

That list of provisions appears to include everything possible to protect accused persons. Yet many of the provisions applied only in Federal cases and were of no value at all in state courts. "Due process of law" is a phrase open to endless interpretations. The same is true of "excessive" bail or fines, and "cruel and unusual" punishment. As an example of the last, the Supreme Court abolished the death penalty in 1972 in *Furman* v. *Georgia,* but at the time of this writing, some state legislatures are planning to try to make it legal again. There is particularly strong feeling about those cases in which policemen and prison guards are killed. But many still believe that death is certainly a "cruel and unusual punishment" and is not justified under *any* circumstances.

Although the right to the assistance of counsel has always been a provision of the Bill of Rights, until recently it was, in actual practice, the right only of those who could afford to pay for it. It was also limited to those who knew about it, since many accused persons were uninformed or illiterate and had no notion of any of their rights.

In addition, such persons were often tricked or frightened into making confessions — whether guilty or innocent — before they ever got as far as a trial. The rights of the accused, then, looked better on paper than they did in life.

The passage of the Fourteenth Amendment in 1868 was of some help. It supposedly brought the provisions of "due process of law" to the states, but there were still loopholes; and in any case, "due process" was still an unclear phrase. In many instances, when rights cases came before the Supreme

Court, the Court permitted the states to make their own decisions.

At last, during the eventful decade of the Sixties, sweeping changes, like brisk winds scattering clouds, clarified the rights of the accused. The first big breakthrough, *Mapp* v. *Ohio*, was soon followed by *Gideon* v. *Wainwright* in 1963.

Clarence Earl Gideon was still another of those "not very nice people" who seem to figure so prominently in rights legislation. He had never been guilty of any serious crime, but had been arrested from time to time for minor offenses and had been in and out of jails. On this occasion, he was arrested because a man named Cook claimed to have seen him leaving the Bay Harbor Poolroom in Florida, at five-thirty one morning. Investigation showed that a window of the poolroom had been smashed and its cigarette machine and jukebox broken into and robbed. Gideon was accused of the crime; he had no money and no lawyer, and so he conducted his own defense. Several persons testified in his behalf, but since Gideon lacked the skill of a lawyer in questioning witnesses, they weren't of much value. Mr. Cook (who much later appeared to be the guilty party!) testified against him, and Gideon was convicted and sentenced to five years in jail.

Unlike many other prisoners, this one had spent

enough time in courts and jails to know that the Sixth Amendment granted him the right to counsel, and he had reminded the judge of that fact before his trial had begun. The judge, however, informed Gideon that in the State of Florida free legal services were provided only in cases involving the death penalty. In all other cases, it was up to the accused to hire a lawyer if he could pay for one. Gideon felt that he had lost his case because he couldn't pay.

With a rather remarkable show of knowledge, Gideon appealed to the Supreme Court, following all of the proper rules of procedure, insisting that the Sixth Amendment guaranteed his right to counsel and that it ought to apply to the State of Florida under the Fourteenth Amendment. He claimed that he had been deprived of his rights only because he was poor. The lengthy appeal was painstakingly written out in pencil on lined prison paper; and because the Court felt that the issue was a valid one, it agreed to hear the case.

Gideon resulted in the great landmark decision that the Fourteenth *did* entitle every American to the right to counsel whether or not he could pay the fee. In the words of Justice Black, "In our adversary system of criminal justice any person hailed into court who is too poor to hire a lawyer, cannot be assured a fair trial unless counsel is provided for him." Clarence Gideon was freed (after two years in jail) because he had had no lawyer, because he was poor, and because he had the determination to fight for his rights against all odds. It was established, thenceforth, that all states must provide free counsel for indigent defendants in all cases involving serious crimes.

Gideon solved one important rights problem, and soon, *Escobedo* v. *Illinois*, 1964, took care of another. It had been in January, 1960, that Danny Escobedo, a twenty-two-year-old laborer from Chicago, was arrested without a warrant. He was taken to the police station for questioning in the fatal shooting of his brother-in-law.

The questioning went on for a long time, but Escobedo was so tense and frightened that he was virtually speechless; as a result, he did not answer any of the questions. In the meantime, his mother had learned that he was in the police station and she called a lawyer, Warren Wolfson. The lawyer immediately obtained a writ of *habeas corpus* and Danny was released and went home.

But only a week and a half later, he was arrested again. This time, Danny's sister, Grace, the widow of the murdered man, and two friends, Benedict Di Gerlando and Bobby Chan, had also been picked up for questioning.

On the trip back to the station house, Danny, hands chained behind his back, was told by one of the policemen that Di Gerlando had said that Danny Escobedo was the murderer. The prisoner answered, "I am sorry but I would like to have advice from my lawyer."

Shortly after the group arrived at the police station, the lawyer did indeed arrive, having been summoned once again by Mrs. Escobedo. But when he told the officer on duty that he had come to see the accused, the officer said, "Danny doesn't know you." Mr. Wolfson remained in the building until one o'clock in the morning, periodically repeating his request to see his client. Finally, seeing that it was hopeless, he gave up and left.

But all during that time, Danny was being questioned — and tricked. As he explained it later, a Spanish-speaking officer had told him, "My sister and I could go home if I pinned it on Benedict Di Gerlando . . . we would go home and be held only as witnesses . . . that we would be able to go home that night . . ."

At one time, Escobedo and Di Gerlando were brought face to face in the same room. According to the testimony of one of the officers, Escobedo, in answer to Di Gerlando's calling *him* the murderer, said, "I didn't shoot Manuel, you did it."

With just this simple statement, Danny Escobedo became deeply involved in a serious crime. For under Illinois law, knowing about a murder without reporting it, or having any connection with the event at all, made him just as guilty as if he had been the one to pull the trigger. But Escobedo didn't know anything about that law because no one had told him. Nor did anyone tell him that he had the right to remain completely silent. He had done so accidentally the first time, but this time he feared that such failure to cooperate would get him into more trouble. And so he continued to answer a series of carefully planned questions, delivered in rapid-fire fashion. His recorded answers amounted to a confession of the crime.

Danny, his sister, and both friends, were all indicted for murder (two of them were later freed), and Escobedo was sentenced to twenty years in prison.

His counsel appealed in Illinois with no result, and only after Danny had spent four and a half years in the penitentiary did the matter come before the Supreme Court. The Court's decision was that in order to uphold the Fifth Amendment to the Constitution, Escobedo should have been *told* that he had the right to refuse to answer and that anything he said could be used against him. He had been allowed, out of ignorance, to act as a witness against himself, and so the "confession" he had made while his lawyer was barred from the room was invalid. Escobedo's conviction was reversed and since there was no longer any evidence against him, he was freed.

This ruling of the Court became a strong reinforcement to *Gideon*. *Escobedo* makes the right to counsel begin during the *interrogation* of an accused person, not in the courtroom. The old and evil practice of obtaining confessions by trickery, ignorance, threats, or torture was legally a thing of the past — except for just one more loophole.

The right to counsel during questioning was now established, but there was still the possibility that prisoners wouldn't know they had such a right and so would fail to ask for a lawyer. The loophole was plugged by *Miranda* v. *Arizona,* 1966.

Ernesto A. Miranda was a truckdriver in Phoenix, Arizona. He was arrested for the kidnapping and rape of an eighteen-year-old girl and was convicted of the crime. He had been identified by the girl, questioned by the police for two hours, and then he had signed a confession. He was sentenced to twenty to thirty years in prison.

Miranda's lawyer appealed the case, and when it reached the Supreme Court, it served to tie up the loose ends that had been left out by *Escobedo*. The

Court threw out the confession that had been made without the presence of a defense attorney. While it was a great victory for justice and rights, the decision didn't help Miranda personally. Even though the Supreme Court had reversed the lower court's decision, the reversal did not remove the indictment; in effect, the first trial was simply nullified. The evidence against Miranda was so clear that he was reconvicted *without* the use of the confession and had to serve his sentence.

But the effects of *Miranda* for others are far-reaching. Whenever police make an arrest, they must tell the suspected criminal *before* they question him that:

1. He has the right to remain silent;
2. Anything he says may be used against him;
3. He has the right to an attorney before questioning begins;
4. If he cannot afford an attorney, one will be provided without charge;
5. After he has understood his rights, he may proceed without counsel if he prefers;
6. Whether he has counsel or not, he may stop the questioning at any time.

The *Miranda* decision was made only by a 5 to 4 majority. Chief Justice Warren, in favor of the decision, felt that the case raised "questions which go to the very root of our concepts of American criminal jurisprudence," but the controversy in the Court was bitter. The dissenting Justices thought the decision was a dangerous experiment at a time when the crime rate was high, and Mr. Justice Harlan called it a "new doctrine" that reflects "a balance in favor of the accused."

Danny Escobedo disagreed. When told about the *Miranda* decision he said, "I think it was very nice of them. Something good."

Miranda, like *Gideon,* applied only to those accused of serious crimes; it made no provision for misdemeanors — relatively minor crimes which usually carry light sentences. But in June of 1972, the protection of rights was granted to *all* offenders with the Supreme Court's *Argersinger* decision.

Jon Richard Argersinger had been convicted, in Florida, of carrying a concealed weapon, a misdemeanor in that state. He was sentenced to pay a fine of five hundred dollars or serve a jail sentence of three months.

On his appeal, the Court agreed unanimously to extend the guarantees of the Sixth Amendment, the right to counsel, to misdemeanor cases as well as to more serious ones. *No one* may be sentenced to jail unless he has had the assistance of counsel, or has been offered assistance and refused.

Critics of the decision have said that the ruling would place an intolerable burden on already over-burdened defense lawyers. There cannot possibly be enough of them to serve the four to five million misdemeanor cases (excluding traffic cases) that jam the courts each year. Misdemeanors vary in different states and range all the way from spitting in public places, to drunkenness, to indecent exposure.

Mr. Justice Douglas has pointed out that the burden on lawyers would be eased if there were fewer prosecutions for those crimes which are "victimless." He also noted that if a judge decides beforehand that he will not impose a jail sentence for a minor offense, he will not have to assign a lawyer. He concluded that the help of a lawyer was a "fundamental right, where an accused is deprived of liberty."

Few Americans would take exception to that. Our Constitutional rights extend to the poor, the ignorant, and the corrupt just as they do to the wealthy, the powerful, and the educated. In the words of Justice Hugo L. Black: *"The worst citizen no less than the best is entitled to equal protection of the laws of his state and of his nation."*

Southern drinking facilities, early 1960's

Separate
Is Not
Equal

No State shall . . . deny to any person within its jurisdiction the equal protection of the laws.

AMENDMENT XIV

THE STRUGGLE FOR civil rights for minorities, especially for the black people in this country, is an excellent illustration of the continuing tension between the ideals of the Bill of Rights and the reality of human behavior. When, toward the end of the Civil War, President Lincoln issued his famous Emancipation Proclamation, not a single slave was freed. Like the Declaration of Independence before it, it was an announcement, not a law, and the slaves were actually set free only when the Thirteenth Amendment was added to the Constitution in 1865.

Even then, the people who had been slaves were

still not citizens; that is, they were not entitled to the privileges and protection of the law. They gained citizenship through the Fourteenth Amendment in 1866, which meant to ensure that the privileges of citizenship would be shared equally by all Americans. Aimed pointedly at the Southern states where the freedmen were without civil rights, the Fourteenth said that "no State shall . . . abridge the privileges or immunities of citizens of the United States; nor shall any State deprive any person of life, liberty, or property without due process of law; nor deny to any person . . . the equal protection of the laws."

At first, the Southern states were deeply disturbed by the passage of this amendment because they felt that they would lose control over their own affairs and be forced to treat the freedmen as equals. Their fears were groundless.

Within a pitifully short time, the strong sentiment for equality that had so motivated the North abated, and in many cases, black people were treated no better in the North than in the South. Within a few years, the North and South had begun to settle the differences between them. One of the big differences had been the question of equality for blacks, and the issue was more or less ignored now. The white nation began to knit together once more, with blacks the losers.

Sensitive, as always, to the prevailing mood of the society, the Supreme Court made a series of decisions that upheld states' rights and white supremacy, and in so doing, made a virtual farce of the Fourteenth Amendment. The amendment made so little difference in the life of the nation, that the furor its passage had created soon died down completely.

The section that granted "equal protection of the laws" was obeyed by the South to the letter — and disobeyed entirely in spirit. In order to maintain segregation, these states adopted *Jim Crow*, a system whereby blacks were provided with housing, schools, churches, transportation, and other facilities that were all separate from white facilities, but supposedly equal. In fact, they were usually dramatically *un*equal.

The Fifteenth Amendment, ratified in 1870, gave freedmen the right to vote. But again, the South sidestepped the spirit of the law by imposing taxes, which most blacks were too poor to pay, and written tests, which the unschooled, often illiterate blacks could not pass. In addition, Southern whites made it plain to blacks that to show up at the polls was to risk a beating. The net result was that even though they now had the Constitutional right to vote, blacks were effectively barred from doing so throughout the South and in some parts of the North. Incidentally, the Fifteenth Amendment applied chiefly to black *males* because, except in a few states, no woman, black or white, had the right to vote until that right was granted by the Nineteenth Amendment in 1920.

So once again, laws that looked perfectly adequate on paper, did little to change the facts. In spite of the civil rights amendments that followed the Civil War, the freedmen never had an opportunity to gain true equality. Poor schools, poor housing, poor jobs, discrimination of every sort, took their toll. In 1970, a century after the Emancipation, the census showed that while one out of ten white persons was poor, nearly one out of three black persons was poor — and deprived socially as well as financially. In 1963, President John F. Kennedy told the nation:

> The Negro baby born in America today, regardless of the section of the Nation in which he is born, has about one-half as much chance of completing high school as a white baby born in the same place on the same day, one-third as much chance of completing college, one-third as much chance of becoming a professional man, twice as much chance of becoming unemployed, about one-seventh as much chance of earning $10,000 a year, a life expectancy which is seven years shorter, and the prospects of earning only half as much.

Blacks are not the only Americans who have failed to receive the equal protection promised by the

Constitution. Indians, Mexicans, Puerto Ricans, students, and women of all races and backgrounds are among the minority groups still struggling for equality. While the struggles continue, the last decade or two have seen more progress than all the years that went before, but some of it was dearly bought with blood, tears, and human life.

Although minor advances in civil rights were made from time to time, it was chiefly during the 1960's that twenty-three million black Americans actually smashed some of the Jim Crow barriers that had existed for so long.

The first rumblings of the storm to come had begun back in the Fifties, when a little black girl named Linda Carol Brown stood on a cold street corner waiting for a school bus. Linda was eight years old, and she boarded the bus at seven forty each morning to travel to an all-black school that was twenty-one blocks from her home in Topeka, Kansas. It didn't take very long for the bus to get to the school—but when it arrived, the children had to stand outside, no matter what the weather, until the school opened at nine o'clock.

Linda Carol's father and some other black parents tried to enroll their children in the perfectly good school that was only seven blocks from home, but they were told that it was impossible because that

school was for white children only. The parents
went to court with the complaint that they were
being denied equal protection of the laws under the
Fourteenth Amendment.

The case, *Brown* v. *Board of Education of Topeka,
Kansas,* reached the Supreme Court in 1954. It had
been grouped with several other cases, and the
blacks were represented by Thurgood Marshall of
the National Association for the Advancement of
Colored People (NAACP), who in 1967, became the
first black to sit on the Supreme Court.

In a historic decision that marked the beginning
of the major civil rights battle to come, the Court
ruled that segregated schools were unconstitutional.
The entire fabric of Southern education was doomed
to destruction when Chief Justice Warren wrote:
*"We conclude that in the field of public education the
doctrine of 'separate but equal' has no place. Separate
educational facilities are inherently unequal."*

In an effort to smooth over some of the strife that
was sure to erupt in the South, the Supreme Court
was slow to insist that its ruling be obeyed. After a
year, however, the Court ordered that school segregation be brought to an end "with all deliberate speed."
The South dug in its heels and prepared to fight.

Even though school boards in a few communities
tried to be cooperative, segregationists were quick to
defeat their efforts. In some places, all of the white

children were withdrawn from schools and sent to private schools instead; in other areas, open violence flared.

A crisis was reached in Little Rock, Arkansas, in 1957, when the first nine black students were about to enroll in all-white Central High School. Governor Orval E. Faubus sent National Guard units to keep the young people from entering the school. For three weeks, armed men kept the black students out of the building. Finally, under court order, the guardsmen were withdrawn, but now the girls and boys had to be protected by policemen from a furious white mob that surrounded them as they finally entered the high school.

The situation was so desperate that two days later, on September 24th, President Eisenhower sent a thousand paratroopers to Little Rock to keep the peace. The students were able to finish the term, and the school was finally integrated — but not before Governor Faubus had closed *all* of the high schools in the State of Arkansas for one full year.

In 1962, James Meredith became the first black student to enroll at the University of Mississippi. The riots that surrounded his appearance there took the lives of two men. President Kennedy ordered sixteen thousand troops to the scene to prevent further violence.

Similar events took place throughout the decade

and even beyond it. There were disturbances in the
North, too, where all-black schools existed in many
areas not because the schools were intentionally
segregated, but because the housing patterns were.
School authorities attempted to integrate the schools
by transporting children by bus from one neighborhood to another. White parents often objected, sometimes strenuously, and there were ugly scenes as
parents actually harassed black children as they
arrived at formerly white schools. If there is any note
of hope in such a situation, it is that the white *children* made no objection to the newcomers; it was
only some of the parents who did.

In 1968, sixty-eight percent of black children
were still attending all-black schools in eleven
Southern states. The Supreme Court once again
issued strong orders, but they were made totally
ineffectual by a yielding attitude on the part of
President Nixon who was apparently eager to win
the votes of Southern white segregationists for the
1972 election. His chief weapon was his opposition
to busing, the only means to integration in many
areas.

Still, in spite of the obstacles, there was progress
made, with a few notable strongholds of segregation
moving more slowly than the rest. One of the worst
cities in the South was Memphis, Tennessee, where,

in January, 1973, eighty-eight percent of black children still attended all-black schools, although a busing program was about to begin. This was twelve years after the Memphis school desegregation plan had officially started.

While desegregation was gradually becoming a reality in schools, it was making headway in other aspects of American life as well. Transportation became integrated after the Montgomery bus boycott of 1955 was followed by persistent groups of Freedom Riders. A sit-in that began at a Woolworth's lunch counter in North Carolina in 1960 paved the road to desegregation in restaurants and other public facilities. Similarly, advances have been made in housing, with many blacks moving into formerly all-white suburbs, buying real estate, and renting apartments in buildings which had excluded them earlier.

The decade saw the birth of SNCC, first under the leadership of Stokely Carmichael and later, H. Rap Brown. It saw the reemergence of CORE, which, under the leadership of James Farmer, rose to new vigor.

Blacks were banding together, and in their unity they began to feel their strength. Dr. Martin Luther King, Jr., who founded the Southern Christian Leadership Conference to bring about change without violence, was unquestionably one of the great influences of the era.

While many leaders had their followers, none had such a following as Dr. King. In the spring of 1963, he organized a mass demonstration in Birmingham, Alabama, to protest segregation there. The demonstrators were threatened, cursed at, soaked with firehoses, set upon by dogs, and harassed by policemen. They demonstrated just the same — peaceably.

Then in August of the same year, Dr. King led a peaceful "March on Washington for Jobs and Freedom." Nearly a quarter million Americans, both black and white, jammed into Washington, D. C., by plane, train, car, and bus, to participate. Dr. King thrilled the marchers and the nation with a speech that told of his dream for America:

> . . . let freedom ring . . . to speed up that day when all of God's children, black and white men, Jews and Gentiles, Protestants and Catholics, will be able to join hands and sing . . . "Free at last! Free at last! Thank God Almighty, we are free at last!"

Dr. King was senselessly and tragically assassinated in 1968, but not before he saw the first few fruits of his labors: on July 2, 1964, President Johnson had signed a Civil Rights Act into law. While the provisions were not new, the fact that they were carefully spelled out, without loopholes, ambiguities, or unclear language, was.

The Civil Rights Act of 1964 prohibited the use of Federal funds in any projects that practiced discrimination; it ruled out discrimination in places of public accommodation or recreation and in all resorts — which included such facilities as buses, trains, hotels, restaurants, theaters, sports arenas, swimming pools, beaches, and so forth; it put an end to job discrimination and to different standards for black and white voters.

The Twenty-fourth Amendment, which also went into effect in 1964, abolished the poll tax in Federal elections so that no citizen could be denied the right to vote because he couldn't afford to pay a tax. In 1966, the Supreme Court ruled in *Harper* v. *Virginia State Board of Elections* that *all* poll taxes, in local as well as Federal elections, were illegal.

The Voting Rights Act of 1965 took care of the other bars to black votes. It did away with "special" (discriminatory) literacy tests amd made any kind of interference with voters a crime. At the time that the act became law, only a little over forty-three percent of the eligible blacks were registered to vote in the eleven Southern states. By 1970, Southern black registration had already passed the sixty percent mark.

In the meantime, although civil rights were expanding, progress was much too slow for many blacks who had lost all patience waiting for the promise of full equality to become a reality. The new laws, while good, may even have added to the discontent because they were at odds with the unemployment, poor jobs, ghettos, and poverty that blacks had to contend with. Militant groups such as the Black Panther Party emerged and urged violence rather than the doctrine of peaceful persuasion so dear to Martin Luther King, Jr.

Under dynamic leaders like Huey P. Newton, Bobby Seale, and Eldridge Cleaver, Panthers made an impact on the black community by preaching Black Power; they aroused racial pride with the slogan "Black Is Beautiful." For the first time in America, blacks were urged to stop imitating whites, to adopt African dress, wear Afro hairstyles, to learn African history and languages.

Black Power meant the opposite of integration. It stood for *black* business enterprises, black *communities, black* literature and art. Many white liberals who had devoted themselves to the cause of equal rights, felt that now blacks were discriminating against whites and harming the rights campaign. White segregationists were simply angry and outraged.

Outbreaks of unrest and discontent led to violence and looting, and finally, to great riots in Watts, Cleveland, Detroit, Chicago, and other cities. Whites and blacks were separated to opposite sides of the battlelines and the spirit of American union seemed doomed for a time.

Both black militants and white and black policemen were shot and killed before some stability began to return. In 1969, just before the turn of what had been an uncommonly eventful decade, *Newsweek* magazine printed the results of a poll that had been conducted for them by the Gallup Organization. It showed that twenty-one percent of the blacks polled would have liked to establish a separate black nation within the United States; seventy-four percent preferred to live in an integrated neighborhood; and seventy-eight percent wanted to send their children to integrated schools.

The great majority, then, still shared Dr. King's dream of black and white men joining hands to sing "Free at last!" By the beginning of the seventies, it looked as if the first steps toward the dream had been taken. A sprinkling of black mayors had been elected to office in cities across the nation. We had one black senator, thirteen congressmen, and eight hundred other elected black officials. Then, in the 1972 elections, there were 598 blacks elected to office in the eleven Southern states alone; by February, 1973, the Voter Education Project reported that 1,148 public offices in the South were held by blacks.

It was heartening to note that in the city of Selma, Alabama, where nonviolent demonstrators had been brutally attacked by policemen in 1965, half of the ten City Council seats went to blacks. No black had held an elected office in 1965, and black voter registration at that time was 2.3 percent of those eligible to vote; in 1972, it was sixty-seven percent.

Black incomes were rising, too — not fast enough, but faster than white incomes. Perhaps the worst of the struggle for civil rights — rights that had long been granted on paper — was over and America would indeed see the day when all men were really equal and the nation would "live out the true meaning of its creed."

Although our Constitution with its Bill of Rights was a truly remarkable document, we have seen that it was virtually useless to black Americans for almost two hundred years, since segregationists were able to obey the letter of the law while totally ignoring its spirit. Now, at last, the spirit and the letter were drawing closer together — not one as yet, but surely closer than ever before.

Women demonstrating for equal rights

Equality
for
All

BLACK RIGHTS were not the only ones to improve between the 1960's and the 1970's. Although largely unofficial, attitudes have definitely begun to shift toward equal rights for such special groups as homosexuals and such broad groups as students and children.

We saw that in the *Tinker* case in 1969, the Court declared that "students do not shed their constitutional rights at the schoolhouse gate." In another case a few years earlier there had been a similar decision; in 1965, in Arizona, a boy named Gerald Gault made an obscene telephone call to a woman.

If Gerald had been an adult, the maximum jail sentence for this offense would have been two months, but Gerald was fifteen and he was committed to a state school to remain until he was twenty-one — a period of six years. After two years, the Supreme Court granted him his freedom stating that "neither the Fourteenth Amendment nor the Bill of Rights is for adults alone."

While this was certainly an important statement, it did not lead to any clear-cut laws that deal with the rights of minors. The prevailing attitude was that parents know best, and in a sense, are the law. This is not always reasonable since some parents are irresponsible, incompetent, or even cruel and inhuman.

Among the many rights denied to children are the right to institute lawsuits or the right to get working papers without the permission of a parent. An adopted child has no right to his family records.

It has also traditionally been impossible for children to seek medical treatment without a parent's permission, but this is an area in which we are beginning to see change; most states now permit minors to seek help for venereal disease without the parents' knowledge. Similarly, at least two states, Massachusetts and Michigan, permit children as young as thirteen to be treated for drug problems confidentially, and at least two states — New York and Florida — place no age or consent restrictions on abortion.

The entire area of children's rights is a relatively new one. While not very much of a concrete nature has been accomplished as yet, there is a growing group of people who intend to see to it that it becomes an area of wide public concern.

A rights movement which *has* had wide — although not total — acceptance is women's liberation. It is already difficult to recall that, not many years ago, some people were startled to learn that not all women thought that raising a family was a woman's only true calling, and that, in fact, woman's place was not necessarily in the home. While there was always a sprinkling of women in professions, recent years have seen a genuinely sharp rise in the number of female professionals, executives, and holders of public office.

Although we tend to think of the women's liberation movement as a separate and independent entity, it was not; it was, rather, an outgrowth of the civil rights movement, of the general ferment for rights and equality that bubbled to the surface of every segment of society during the sixties.

We also tend to think of the struggle for women's rights as something relatively new and revolutionary in our own time, but in fact, the struggle has a venerable history that started well over a century ago.

Periods of upheaval have occurred with some regularity during the years of our country's existence; one such period came along during the 1820's, and this time, the upheaval centered around a mass zeal for reform. Social and moral uplift were the great goals of the day. Large numbers of prominent clergymen, writers, and philosophers envisioned a new and better society without poverty, without violence or crime; "do-gooders" sprang forth from everywhere to seek better treatment for the poor, for criminals, and for the mentally ill. Since many of society's troubles at this time were blamed on drunkenness, the temperance movement gained strength quickly and soon achieved prominence all over the nation. In 1826, a number of local societies joined to form the American Society for the Promotion of Temperance. Large numbers of women were attracted to the aims of the society, but when they tried to take an active part in its work, they were rebuffed. Woman's place, they were told, was in the home. The women stayed home but they grew increasingly more unhappy about it.

While every American is well acquainted with the evils of slavery, not all recognize that the status of women in the first half of the nineteenth century was in many respects comparable. As soon as a woman married, she gave up all of her civil rights. She had no control over her own property (even if she had inherited it from her parents), no control over money, and she could not sign any legal papers. She was her husband's charge in all respects and had no recourse if he chose to beat her. She was as lacking in legal rights as an infant, a criminal, or a lunatic.

If a wife worked, her husband was legally entitled to take all of her wages; he was also entitled to custody of the children if he decided to leave her. The husband alone could decide where the family was to live, and when he died, he did not have to leave any part of his property to his wife unless he chose to. If he died without a will, it was the state that decided what the widow should have. New York State made very careful provision for such situations: a widow was entitled to the family Bible, books — up to the value of fifty dollars — spinning wheels, clothing, beds and linens, one table, six chairs, a half dozen each of knives, forks, spoons, cups and saucers, and a few other odds and ends. She inherited neither money nor real estate.

Women had other problems, too. Education was

virtually unavailable to them because they were generally thought to be intellectually inferior to men. If they chose, or were forced to work outside the home, it was at the most menial kind of jobs and for the most meager wages. In addition, they were expected to be subservient and modest at all times, and to have no thought for sexual matters except to beget children or accommodate their husbands. It was no wonder that women were ready to rebel.

In 1840, a World Antislavery Convention was held in London. Several very advanced and "unfeminine" women, including Elizabeth Cady Stanton and Lucretia Mott, attended as delegates, but as in the case of the Temperance Society, they were not permitted to participate in the meetings.

The women went home, but they went home angry and determined to act. It took them a while, but in 1848, they called a Women's Rights Convention at Seneca Falls, New York. Two hundred and fifty women attended, and they issued a document which was patterned closely on the Declaration of Independence. They called it *The Declaration of Sentiments and Resolutions* and it stated in part:

> The history of mankind is a history of repeated injuries and usurpations on the part of man toward woman, having in direct object the establish-

ment of an absolute tyranny over her. To prove this, let facts be submitted to a candid world.

He has never permitted her to exercise her inalienable right to the elective franchise.

He has made her, if married, in the eyes of the law civilly dead.

He has taken from her all rights to property, even to the wages she earns. . . .

He has denied her the facilities for obtaining a thorough education — all colleges being closed against her. . . .

He has created a false public sentiment, by giving to the world a different code of morals for men and women, by which moral delinquencies which exclude women from society are not only tolerated but deemed of little account in man. . . .

He has endeavored, in every way that he could, to destroy her confidence in her own powers, to lessen her self-respect, and to make her willing to lead a dependent and abject life.

Like the Declaration of Independence before it, this powerful statement had no immediate impact; it needed some time.

Although Mount Holyoke College for Women had actually opened its doors in 1837 and Oberlin College became coeducational in the same year, it was several decades before even a few more educational institutions became available to women.

Gains were made, one at a time, to give women their legal rights, at about the same snail's pace through the period from 1848 and into the 1880's. In 1883, Susan B. Anthony travelled abroad to spread the message of rights for women, and the movement began to gain ground internationally. In this country, once property rights for women were established, the main focus of the struggle was on women's suffrage — the right to vote. It remained the primary issue until the Nineteenth Amendment was ratified in 1920.

Now, once again, women could turn their attention to other matters. They wanted better jobs, higher pay, the right to live alone without creating a scandal, to smoke and drink if they chose, and especially, they wanted the right to birth control. In this era of the double standard of sexual morality and hypocritical prudery, the women who spoke out publicly on the issue were true heroines.

Outstanding among them was Margaret Sanger, a courageous woman who militated for free advice and instruction in birth control for all women. Considered a dangerous radical by many, she had joined with another "radical," Emma Goldman, in 1915 to form the National Birth Control League which attempted to lift the restrictions on birth-control education that existed under the Comstock Law. In 1916, Mrs. Sanger, a nurse, actually opened a birth-control clinic in Brooklyn and was promptly jailed for thirty days as a result.

As soon as she was released she began to travel and to lecture on her topic and, in 1920, she again opened a clinic. This time, the police raided the premises and confiscated all of the medical records. It was not until 1936 that it became legal to dispense information on birth control in the United States — and the practice was not officially endorsed by the American Medical Association until 1937.

While it is true that women had gained the right to vote in 1920, and many entered college and professional fields soon after, not only did they never approach equality with men, they actually lost ground after the initial thrust. In 1960, a smaller proportion of women to men were earning college degrees than had in 1930, and their incomes, compared to men in the same kind of jobs, declined. Women were *still* generally acknowledged to be essentially wives and mothers. They still belonged at home and needed to be protected and supported by men. Women who were not were usually objects of society's pity.

As late as 1970, with women constituting more than fifty percent of the population, only 7.6 percent of the nation's doctors were women, and a mere one percent of those were surgeons; women accounted for one percent of the architects, 2.8 percent of lawyers, nine percent of the full professors. There was one woman federal appeals court judge out of a total of ninety-seven, and four federal district court judges out of 402. Seven percent of employed women earned more than $10,000 as opposed to forty percent of the men. The main professions for women were still nursing, librarianship, and teaching. The biggest single employer of women was the telephone company, but until recent legislation forced the issue, women held no important executive positions in the Bell System.

In 1961, President Kennedy set up a Commission on the Status of Women to study discrimination, and at about the same time, women began to band together in such action organizations as NOW, the National Organization for Women. They agitated for child-care centers, equal pay for equal work, equal job opportunity, equal education and professional status, the right to birth-control information and care, and the right to abortion.

"Consciousness-raising" or discussion groups, in which women shared their feelings and talked about their common problems and the means of solving them became more numerous. Women, it turned out, did not all want to remain weak and dependent; a great many of them wanted equality with men, wanted to join with them in truly egalitarian family relationships and become their equals in professional and social life.

The movement gained ground swiftly, and in

spite of some noisy resistance, within a decade large numbers of both men and women were embracing the correctness of the equality policy.

Laws were passed which forbade any kind of job discrimination against women; women were to receive equal opportunity and equal pay with men. To date, these laws have been poorly enforced. In July, 1973, witnesses testifying before the Joint Economic Committee — a Congressional committee studying the economic status of women — made a number of charges. Among them:

Less than half of the back pay that is due women because of violations of the laws governing equal pay and fair labor standards, is ever paid.

The Equal Employment Opportunity Commission which handles discrimination cases, completes about fifteen thousand cases a year; it presently has a backlog of sixty-five thousand cases and this figure is expected to rise to ninety thousand next year.

Some government departments — including the Department of Labor — do not observe the anti-discriminatory regulations themselves.

The Office of Federal Contract Compliance, which makes sure that government contractors do not discriminate, has no women in executive positions in any of its own offices.

There were many other charges made as well —

but with growing awareness of the problems, and continuing pressure on legislators, there is little question that progress will be made.

In other areas, new laws have given women better legal status in matters of property; discrimination against women in restaurants ("Men Only" signs at lunch), in applications for credit, and in housing, has ended. In many homes, fathers have learned to diaper the baby, cook the dinner, and take over a varying share of the household chores. This kind of reversal of the old set roles and patterns was extremely rare until the 1960's. The fact that it now exists commonly — and almost invariably among college-educated younger families — is due largely to the growth of women's rights.

Not unexpectedly, women's rights make for men's rights, too; any thinking man would rather have a genuine mate than a helpless dependent. And, of course, if the new mores make for happier women, they make for happier families, and everybody stands to gain.

As this book goes to press, the Equal Rights Amendment, which states that "equality of rights under the law shall not be denied or abridged by the United States or by any state on account of sex," is still pending. It was approved by the Senate in March, 1972, but so far it has not been either accepted or rejected by enough states to determine its fate. If ratified, the bill will become the Twenty-seventh Amendment to the Constitution.

Perhaps the most dramatic battle of all for women's rights was the one that women waged for the right to plan their families as they chose and to have the right to abortion. This had long been a particularly sensitive area not only for action, but even for discussion in the United States. Most abortions, other than those performed by a doctor to save the life of the mother, were considered criminal acts because they were illegal, and in addition, many states had laws forbidding the sale of birth-control devices, or the dissemination of information on the subject.

The Supreme Court's legalization of abortion in January, 1973 (*Jane Roe* v. *Henry Wade*), demonstrated forcefully how the law follows changing moral and social trends. Few issues had ever created so much controversy as this one, and it is remarkable that a court could decide such an issue at all. There are still rumblings on many outraged fronts, and unquestionably, a major effort will be made, particularly by religious groups, to bring about a reversal of the decision.

That the abortion ruling was made in the first place showed not only how the Court changes with the times, but clearly pointed up once again the flexibility of our Constitution, for in writing the majority opinion Justice Harry A. Blackmun noted:

> The Constitution does not explicitly mention any right of privacy. In a line of decision, however, the Court has recognized that a right of personal privacy, or a guarantee of certain areas or zones of privacy, does exist under the Constitution.
>
> This right of privacy, whether it be founded in the Fourteenth Amendment's concept of personal liberty and restrictions upon state action . . . is broad enough to encompass a woman's decision whether or not to terminate her pregnancy.

This statement, made while disapproval was still rampant in the land, spoke out for freedom and liberty and for American rights. It was important because the life and future of democracy lie in the rights of the people, and each time we strengthen our rights, we add strength to our nation.

We have seen that, sometimes, the rights of the individual conflict with the rights of society; no one has the right to falsely cry "Fire!" in a crowded theater. Similarly, no one has the right to pollute the earth, or to harm in any way the people who inhabit it. No one has the right to break the law. Freedom, like most other things, has its limits.

Knowing where the limits lie can be difficult, although Justice Oliver Wendell Holmes provided a general rule when he said, "The right to swing my fist ends where the other man's nose begins."

The eighteenth-century society that framed our Constitution had its heart in the right place — but its perception of where the limits of freedom lay was not always clear. Fortunately, the writers left us a flexible document that we could bend and mold in order to achieve freedom and equality for all. It has taken us a long time — too long a time — to go as far as we have toward that end. The ideal is a society without discrimination of any kind, a true democracy founded on equality and brotherhood.

Democracy is the most difficult of systems to maintain. There are always those who, for reasons of ignorance, prejudice, or hope of personal gain, would, if given the opportunity, undermine the rights of others. It is up to every one of us to prevent them from having that opportunity.

Our Constitution is a good one, and we have seen the extent to which the Supreme Court can interpret and manipulate it. Therefore, if we are to continue to move in the direction of ideal democracy, it is essential to have a Supreme Court that shares our goals. We have no power to select our Justices, but we *can* select the President who does. Every citizen who goes to the polls on election day is directing the future course of civil rights. A President who believes in the rights of the people will appoint Justices who will probably further them; a President who believes in the centralization of power will appoint Justices who he believes — or hopes — will curtail rights whenever possible.

We citizens of a democracy have to be more thoughtful than people who live under any other system, for in effect, we govern ourselves. It isn't easy — but then, no one ever promised us that it *would* be.

Back in 1787, when the Constitutional Convention had just ended, a woman approached Benjamin Franklin and said, "What have you given us, Dr. Franklin — a monarchy, an aristocracy, or a republic?" Without hesitation, Franklin replied, "A republic, madam — if you can keep it!"

The Declaration of Independence*

*The unanimous Declaration of the
thirteen united States of America.*

WHEN IN THE COURSE of human events it becomes necessary
for one people to dissolve the political bands which have con-
nected them with another, and to assume among the Powers of
the earth, the separate and equal station to which the Laws of
Nature and of Nature's God entitle them, a decent respect to the
opinions of mankind requires that they should declare the causes
which impel them to the separation.

We hold these truths to be self-evident, that all men are created
equal, that they are endowed by their Creator with certain unalienable Rights, that among these are Life, Liberty and the pursuit of Happiness. That to secure these rights, Governments are
instituted among Men, deriving their just Powers from the consent
of the governed. That whenever any Form of Government becomes
destructive of these ends, it is the Right of the People to alter or to

---

* Reprinted from the facsimile of the engrossed copy in the National Archives.
The original spelling, capitalization, and punctuation have been retained. Para-
graphing has been added.

abolish it, and to institute new Government, laying its foundation on such principles and organizing its Powers in such form, as to them shall seem most likely to effect their Safety and Happiness. Prudence, indeed, will dictate that Governments long established should not be changed for light and transient causes; and accordingly all experience hath shewn, that mankind are more disposed to suffer, while evils are sufferable, than to right themselves by abolishing the forms to which they are accustomed. But when a long train of abuses and usurpations, pursuing invariably the same Object evinces a design to reduce them under absolute Despotism, it is their right, it is their duty, to throw off such Government, and to provide new Guards for their future security. Such has been the patient sufferance of these Colonies; and such is now the necessity which constrains them to alter their former Systems of Government. The history of the present King of Great Britain is a history of repeated injuries and usurpations, all having in direct object the establishment of an absolute Tyranny over these States. To prove this, let Facts be submitted to a candid world.

He has refused his Assent to Laws, the most wholesome and necessary for the public good.

He has forbidden his Governors to pass Laws of immediate and pressing importance, unless suspended in their operation till his Assent should be obtained; and when so suspended, he has utterly neglected to attend to them.

He has refused to pass other Laws for the accommodation of large districts of people, unless those people would relinquish the right of Representation in the Legislature, a right inestimable to them and formidable to tyrants only.

He has called together legislative bodies at places unusual, uncomfortable, and distant from the depository of their Public Records, for the sole Purpose of fatiguing them into compliance with his measures.

He has dissolved Representative Houses repeatedly, for opposing with manly firmness his invasions on the rights of the People.

He has refused for a long time, after such dissolutions, to cause others to be elected; whereby the Legislative Powers, incapable of Annihilation, have returned to the People at large for their exercise; the State remaining in the mean time exposed to all the dangers of invasion from without, and convulsions within.

He has endeavoured to prevent the Population of these States; for that purpose obstructing the Laws for Naturalization of Foreigners; refusing to pass others to encourage their migrations hither, and raising the conditions of new Appropriations of Lands.

He has obstructed the Administration of Justice, by refusing his Assent to Laws for establishing Judiciary Powers.

He has made judges dependent on his Will alone, for the tenure of their offices, and the amount and payment of their salaries.

He has erected a multitude of New Offices, and sent hither swarms of Officers to harrass our People, and eat out their substance.

He has kept among us, in times of peace, Standing Armies without the Consent of our legislatures.

He has affected to render the Military independent of and superior to the Civil Power.

He has combined with others to subject us to a jurisdiction foreign to our constitution, and unacknowledged by our laws; giving his Assent to their Acts of pretended Legislation:

For Quartering large bodies of armed troops among us:

For protecting them, by a mock Trial, from Punishment for any Murders which they should commit on the Inhabitants of these States:

For cutting off our Trade with all parts of the world:

For imposing Taxes on us without our Consent:

For depriving us in many cases, of the benefits of Trial by Jury:

For transporting us beyond Seas to be tried for pretended offences:

For abolishing the free System of English Laws in a neighbouring Province, establishing therein an Arbitrary government, and enlarging its Boundaries so as to render it at once an example and fit instrument for introducing the same absolute rule into these Colonies:

For taking away our Charters, abolishing our most valuable Laws, and altering fundamentally the Forms of our Governments:

For suspending our own Legislatures, and declaring themselves

THE DECLARATION OF INDEPENDENCE

invested with Power to legislate for us in all cases whatsoever.

He has abdicated Government here, by declaring us out of his Protection, and waging War against us.

He has plundered our seas, ravaged our Coasts, burnt our towns, and destroyed the lives of our people.

He is at this time transporting large Armies of foreign Mercenaries to compleat the works of death, desolation and tyranny, already begun with circumstances of Cruelty and perfidy scarcely paralleled in the most barbarous ages, and totally unworthy the Head of a civilized nation.

He has constrained our fellow Citizens taken Captive on the high Seas to bear Arms against their Country, to become the executioners of their friends and Brethren, or to fall themselves by their Hands.

He has excited domestic insurrections amongst us, and has endeavoured to bring on the inhabitants of our frontiers, the merciless Indian Savages, whose known rule of warfare, is an undistinguished destruction of all ages, sexes and conditions.

In every stage of these Oppressions We have Petitioned for Redress in the most humble terms: Our repeated Petitions have been answered only by repeated injury. A Prince, whose character is thus marked by every act which may define a Tyrant, is unfit to be the ruler of a free People.

Nor have We been wanting in attentions to our Brittish brethren. We have warned them from time to time of attempts by their legislature to extend an unwarrantable jurisdiction over us. We have reminded them of the circumstances of our emigration and settlement here. We have appealed to their native justice and magnanimity, and we have conjured them by the ties of our common kindred to disavow these usurpations, which, would inevitably interrupt our connections and correspondence. They too have been deaf to the voice of justice and of consanguinity. We must, therefore, acquiesce in the necessity, which denounces our Separation, and hold them, as we hold the rest of mankind, Enemies in War, in Peace Friends.

WE, THEREFORE, the Representatives of the UNITED STATES OF AMERICA, in General Congress, Assembled, appealing to the Supreme Judge of the world for the rectitude of our intentions, do, in the Name, and by Authority of the good People of these Colonies, solemnly publish and declare, That these United Colonies are, and of Right ought to be FREE AND INDEPENDENT STATES; that they are Absolved from all Allegiance to the British Crown, and that all political connection between them and the State of Great Britain, is and ought to be totally dissolved; and that, as Free and Independent States, they have full Power to levy War, conclude Peace, contract Alliances, establish Commerce, and to do all other Acts and Things which Independent States may of right do. And for the support of this Declaration, with a firm reliance on the protection of divine Providence, we mutually pledge to each other our Lives, our Fortunes and our sacred Honor.

The Constitution of the United States of America *

WE THE PEOPLE of the United States, in Order to form a more perfect Union, establish Justice, insure domestic Tranquility, provide for the common defence, promote the general Welfare, and secure the Blessings of Liberty to ourselves and our Posterity, do ordain and establish this Constitution for the United States of America.

Article. I.

SECTION. 1. All legislative Powers herein granted shall be vested in a Congress of the United States, which shall consist of a Senate and House of Representatives.

SECTION. 2. The House of Representatives shall be composed of Members chosen every second Year by the People of the several

---

* From the engrossed copy in the National Archives. Original spelling, capitalization, and punctuation have been retained.

THE CONSTITUTION OF THE UNITED STATES

States, and the Electors in each State shall have the Qualifications requisite for Electors of the most numerous Branch of the State Legislature.

No Person shall be a Representative who shall not have attained to the Age of twenty five Years, and been seven Years a Citizen of the United States, and who shall not, when elected, be an Inhabitant of that State in which he shall be chosen.

Representatives and direct Taxes* shall be apportioned among the several States which may be included within this Union, according to their respective Numbers, which shall be determined by adding to the whole Number of free Persons, including those bound to Service for a Term of Years, and excluding Indians not taxed, three fifths of all other Persons.† The actual Enumeration shall be made within three Years after the first Meeting of the Congress of the United States, and within every subsequent Term of ten Years, in such Manner as they shall by Law direct. The Number of Representatives shall not exceed one for every thirty Thousand, but each State shall have at Least one Representative; and until such enumeration shall be made, the State of New Hampshire shall be entitled to chuse three; Massachusetts eight; Rhode Island and Providence Plantations one; Connecticut five; New York six; New Jersey four; Pennsylvania eight; Delaware one; Maryland six; Virginia ten; North Carolina five; South Carolina five; and Georgia three.

When vacancies happen in the Representation from any State, the Executive Authority thereof shall issue Writs of Election to fill such Vacancies.

The House of Representatives shall chuse their Speaker and other Officers; and shall have the sole Power of Impeachment. SECTION. 3. The Senate of the United States shall be composed of two Senators from each State, chosen by the Legislature thereof, for six Years; and each Senator shall have one Vote.‡

Immediately after they shall be assembled in Consequence of the first Election, they shall be divided as equally as may be into three Classes. The Seats of the Senators of the first Class shall

---

* Modified by the Sixteenth Amendment.
† Replaced by the Fourteenth Amendment.
‡ Superseded by the Seventeenth Amendment.

be vacated at the Expiration of the second Year, of the second Class at the Expiration of the fourth Year, and of the third Class at the Expiration of the sixth Year, so that one third may be chosen every second Year; and if Vacancies happen by Resignation, or otherwise, during the Recess of the Legislature of any State, the Executive thereof may make temporary Appointments until the next Meeting of the Legislature, which shall then fill such Vacancies.*

No Person shall be a Senator who shall not have attained to the Age of thirty Years, and been nine Years a Citizen of the United States, and who shall not, when elected, be an Inhabitant of that State for which he shall be chosen.

The Vice President of the United States shall be President of the Senate, but shall have no Vote, unless they be equally divided.

The Senate shall chuse their other Officers, and also a President pro tempore, in the Absence of the Vice President, or when he shall exercise the Office of President of the United States.

The Senate shall have the sole Power to try all Impeachments. When sitting for that Purpose, they shall be on Oath or Affirmation. When the President of the United States is tried, the Chief Justice shall preside: And no Person shall be convicted without the Concurrence of two thirds of the Members present.

Judgment in Cases of Impeachment shall not extend further than to removal from Office, and disqualification to hold and enjoy any Office of honor, Trust or Profit under the United States: but the Party convicted shall nevertheless be liable and subject to Indictment, Trial, Judgment and Punishment, according to Law.

SECTION. 4. The Times, Places and Manner of holding Elections for Senators and Representatives, shall be prescribed in each State by the Legislature thereof, but the Congress may at any time by Law make or alter such Regulation, except as to the Places of chusing Senators.

The Congress shall assemble at least once in every Year, and such Meeting shall be on the first Monday in December, unless they shall by Law appoint a different Day.†

---

* Modified by the Seventeenth Amendment.
† Superseded by the Twentieth Amendment.

THE CONSTITUTION OF THE UNITED STATES

SECTION. 5. Each House shall be the Judge of the Elections, Returns and Qualifications of its own Members, and a Majority of each shall constitute a Quorum to do Business; but a smaller Number may adjourn from day to day, and may be authorized to compel the Attendance of absent Members, in such Manner, and under such Penalties as each House may provide.

Each House may determine the Rules of its Proceedings, punish its Members for disorderly Behaviour, and, with the Concurrence of two thirds, expel a Member.

Each House shall keep a Journal of its Proceedings, and from time to time publish the same, excepting such Parts as may in their Judgment require Secrecy; and the Yeas and Nays of the Members of either House on any question shall, at the Desire of one fifth of those Present, be entered on the Journal.

Neither House, during the Session of Congress, shall, without the Consent of the other, adjourn for more than three days, nor to any other Place than that in which the two Houses shall be sitting.

SECTION. 6. The Senators and Representatives shall receive a Compensation for their Services, to be ascertained by Law, and paid out of the Treasury of the United States. They shall in all Cases, except Treason, Felony and Breach of the Peace, be privileged from Arrest during their Attendance at the Session of their respective Houses, and in going to and returning from the same; and for any Speech or Debate in either House, they shall not be questioned in any other Place.

No Senator or Representative shall, during the Time for which he was elected, be appointed to any civil Office under the Authority of the United States, which shall have been created, or the Emoluments whereof shall have been encreased during such time; and no Person holding any Office under the United States, shall be a Member of either House during his Continuance in Office.

SECTION. 7. All Bills for raising Revenue shall originate in the House of Representatives; but the Senate may propose or concur with Amendments as on other Bills.

Every Bill which shall have passed the House of Representatives and the Senate shall, before it become a Law, be presented to the President of the United States, If he approve he shall sign it, but if not he shall return it, with his Objections to that House in which it shall have originated, who shall enter the Objections at large on their Journal, and proceed to reconsider it. If after such Reconsideration two thirds of that House shall agree to pass the Bill, it shall be sent, together with the Objections, to the other House, by which it shall likewise be reconsidered, and if approved by two thirds of that House, it shall become a Law. But in all such Cases the Votes of both Houses shall be determined by yeas and Nays, and the Names of the Persons voting for and against the Bill shall be entered on the Journal of each House respectively. If any Bill shall not be returned by the President within ten Days (Sundays excepted) after it shall have been presented to him, the Same shall be a Law, in like Manner as if he had signed it, unless the Congress by their Adjournment prevent its Return, in which Case it shall not be a Law.

Every Order, Resolution, or Vote to which the Concurrence of the Senate and House of Representatives may be necessary (except on a question of Adjournment) shall be presented to the President of the United States; and before the Same shall take Effect, shall be approved by him, or being disapproved by him shall be repassed by two thirds of the Senate and House of Representatives, according to the Rules and Limitations prescribed in the Case of a Bill.

SECTION. 8. The Congress shall have Power To lay and collect Taxes, Duties, Imposts and Excises, to pay the Debts and provide for the common Defence and general Welfare of the United States; but all Duties, Imposts and Excises shall be uniform throughout the United States;

To borrow Money on the credit of the United States;

To regulate Commerce with foreign Nations, and among the several States, and with the Indian Tribes;

To establish an uniform Rule of Naturalization, and uniform Laws on the subject of Bankruptcies throughout the United States;

To coin Money, regulate the Value thereof, and of foreign Coin, and fix the Standard of Weights and Measures;

To provide for the Punishment of counterfeiting the Securities and current Coin of the United States;

To establish Post Offices and post Roads;

To promote the Progress of Science and useful Arts, by securing for limited Times to Authors and Inventors the exclusive Right to their respective Writings and Discoveries;

To constitute Tribunals inferior to the supreme Court;

To define and punish Piracies and Felonies committed on the high Seas, and Offences against the Law of Nations;

To declare War, grant Letters of Marque and Reprisal, and make Rules concerning Captures on Land and Water;

To raise and support Armies, but no Appropriation of Money to that Use shall be for a longer Term than two Years;

To provide and maintain a Navy;

To make Rules for the Government and Regulation of the land and naval Forces;

To provide for calling forth the Militia to execute the Laws of the Union, suppress Insurrections and repel Invasions;

To provide for organizing, arming, and disciplining, the Militia, and for governing such Part of them as may be employed in the Service of the United States, reserving to the States respectively, the Appointment of the Officers, and the Authority of training the Militia according to the discipline prescribed by Congress;

To exercise exclusive Legislation in all Cases whatsoever, over such District (not exceeding ten Miles square) as may, by Cession of particular States, and the Acceptance of Congress, become the Seat of the Government of the United States, and to exercise like Authority over all Places purchased by the Consent of the Legislature of the State in which the Same shall be, for the Erection of Forts, Magazines, Arsenals, dock-Yards, and other needful Buildings;—And

To make all Laws which shall be necessary and proper for carrying into Execution the foregoing Powers, and all other Powers vested by this Constitution in the Government of the United States, or in any Department or Officer thereof.

SECTION. 9. The Migration or Importation of such Persons as any of the States now existing shall think proper to admit, shall not be prohibited by the Congress prior to the Year one thousand eight hundred and eight, but a Tax or duty may be imposed on such Importation, not exceeding ten dollars for each Person.

The Privilege of the Writ of Habeas Corpus shall not be suspended, unless when in Cases of Rebellion or Invasion the public

Safety may require it.

No Bill of Attainder or ex post facto Law shall be passed.

No Capitation, or other direct, Tax shall be laid, unless in Proportion to the Census or Enumeration herein before directed to be taken.

No Tax or Duty shall be laid on Articles exported from any State.

No Preference shall be given by any Regulation of Commerce or Revenue to the Ports of one State over those of another: nor shall Vessels bound to, or from, one State, be obliged to enter, clear, or pay Duties in another.

No Money shall be drawn from the Treasury, but in Consequence of Appropriations made by Law, and a regular Statement and Account of the Receipts and Expenditures of all public Money shall be published from time to time.

No Title of Nobility shall be granted by the United States: And no Person holding any Office of Profit or Trust under them, shall, without the Consent of the Congress, accept of any present, Emolument, Office, or Title, of any kind whatever, from any King, Prince, or foreign State.

SECTION. 10. No State shall enter into any Treaty, Alliance, or Confederation; grant Letters of Marque and Reprisal; coin Money; emit Bills of Credit; make any Thing but gold and silver Coin a Tender in Payment of Debts; pass any Bill of Attainder, ex post facto Law, or Law impairing the Obligation of Contracts, or grant any Title of Nobility.

No State shall, without the Consent of the Congress, lay any Imposts or Duties on Imports or Exports, except what may be absolutely necessary for executing it's inspection Laws: and the net Produce of all Duties and Imposts, laid by any State on Imports or Exports, shall be for the Use of the Treasury of the United States; and all such Laws shall be subject to the Revision and Controul of the Congress.

No State shall, without the Consent of Congress, lay any Duty of Tonnage, keep Troops, or Ships of War in time of Peace, enter into any Agreement or Compact with another State, or with a foreign Power, or engage in War, unless actually invaded, or in such imminent Danger as will not admit of delay.

THE CONSTITUTION OF THE UNITED STATES

Article. II.

SECTION. 1. The executive Power shall be vested in a President of the United States of America. He shall hold his Office during the Term of four Years, and, together with the Vice President, chosen for the same Term, be elected, as follows

Each State shall appoint, in such Manner as the Legislature thereof may direct, a Number of Electors, equal to the whole Number of Senators and Representatives to which the State may be entitled in the Congress: but no Senator or Representative, or Person holding an Office of Trust or Profit under the United States, shall be appointed an Elector.

The Electors shall meet in their respective States, and vote by Ballot for two Persons, of whom one at least shall not be an Inhabitant of the same State with themselves. And they shall make a List of all the Persons voted for, and of the Number of Votes for each; which List they shall sign and certify, and transmit sealed to the Seat of the Government of the United States, directed to the President of the Senate. The President of the Senate shall, in the Presence of the Senate and House of Representatives, open all the Certificates, and the Votes shall then be counted. The Person having the greatest Number of Votes shall be the President, if such Number be a Majority of the whole Number of Electors appointed; and if there be more than one who have such Majority, and have an equal Number of Votes, then the House of Representatives shall immediately chuse by Ballot one of them for President; and if no Person have a Majority, then from the five highest on the List the said House shall in like Manner chuse the President. But in chusing the President, the Votes shall be taken by States, the Representation from each State having one Vote; A quorum for this Purpose shall consist of a Member or Members from two thirds of the States, and a Majority of all the States shall be necessary to a Choice. In every Case, after the Choice of the President, the Person having the greatest Number of Votes of the Electors shall be the Vice President. But if there should remain two or more who have equal Votes, the Senate shall chuse from them by Ballot the Vice President.*

---

* Superseded by the Twelfth Amendment.

THE CONSTITUTION OF THE UNITED STATES

The Congress may determine the Time of chusing the Electors, and the Day on which they shall give their Votes; which Day shall be the same throughout the United States.

No Person except a natural born Citizen, or a Citizen of the United States, at the time of the Adoption of this Constitution, shall be eligible to the Office of President, neither shall any Person be eligible to that Office who shall not have attained to the Age of thirty five Years, and been fourteen Years a Resident within the United States.

In Case of the Removal of the President from Office, or of his Death, Resignation, or Inability to discharge the Powers and Duties of the said Office, the Same shall devolve on the Vice President, and the Congress may by Law provide for the Case of Removal, Death, Resignation or Inability, both of the President and Vice President, declaring what Officer shall then act as President, and such Officer shall act accordingly, until the Disability be removed, or a President shall be elected.*

The President shall, at stated Times, receive for his Services, a Compensation, which shall neither be encreased nor diminished during the Period for which he shall have been elected, and he shall not receive within that Period any other Emolument from the United States, or any of them.

Before he enter on the Execution of his Office, he shall take the following Oath or Affirmation:—"I do solemnly swear (or affirm) that I will faithfully execute the Office of President of the United States, and will to the best of my Ability, preserve, protect and defend the Constitution of the United States."

SECTION. 2. The President shall be Commander in Chief of the Army and Navy of the United States, and of the Militia of the several States, when called into the actual Service of the United States; he may require the Opinion, in writing, of the principal Officer in each of the executive Departments, upon any Subject relating to the Duties of their respective Offices, and he shall have Power to grant Reprieves and Pardons for Offences against the United States, except in Cases of Impeachment.

He shall have Power, by and with the Advice and Consent of the Senate, to make Treaties, provided two thirds of the Senators

---

* Modified by the Twenty-fifth Amendment.

present concur; and he shall nominate, and by and with the Advice and Consent of the Senate, shall appoint Ambassadors, other public Ministers and Consuls, Judges of the supreme Court, and all other Officers of the United States, whose Appointments are not herein otherwise provided for, and which shall be established by Law; but the Congress may by Law vest the Appointment of such inferior Officers, as they think proper, in the President alone, in the Courts of Law, or in the Heads of Departments.

The President shall have Power to fill up all Vacancies that may happen during the Recess of the Senate, by granting Commissions which shall expire at the End of their next Session.

SECTION. 3. He shall from time to time give to the Congress Information of the State of the Union, and recommend to their Consideration such Measures as he shall judge necessary and expedient; he may, on extraordinary Occasions, convene both Houses, or either of them, and in Case of Disagreement between them, with Respect to the Time of Adjournment, he may adjourn them to such Time as he shall think proper; he shall receive Ambassadors and other public Ministers; he shall take Care that the Laws be faithfully executed, and shall Commission all the Officers of the United States.

SECTION. 4. The President, Vice President and all civil Officers of the United States, shall be removed from Office on Impeachment for, and Conviction of, Treason, Bribery, or other high Crimes and Misdemeanors.

Article. III.

SECTION. 1. The judicial Power of the United States, shall be vested in one supreme Court, and in such inferior Courts as the Congress may from time to time ordain and establish. The Judges, both of the supreme and inferior Courts, shall hold their Offices during good Behaviour, and shall, at stated Times, receive for their Services, a Compensation, which shall not be diminished during their Continuance in Office.

SECTION. 2. The judicial Power shall extend to all Cases, in Law and Equity, arising under this Constitution, the Laws of the United States, and Treaties made, or which shall be made, under their

Authority;—to all Cases affecting Ambassadors, other public Ministers and Consuls;—to all Cases of admiralty and maritime Jurisdiction;—to Controversies to which the United States shall be a Party;—to Controversies between two or more States;—between a State and Citizens of another State;*—between Citizens of different States,—between Citizens of the same State claiming Lands under Grants of different States, and between a State, or the Citizens thereof, and foreign States, Citizens or Subjects.

In all Cases affecting Ambassadors, other public Ministers and Consuls, and those in which a State shall be Party, the supreme Court shall have original Jurisdiction. In all the other Cases before mentioned, the supreme Court shall have appellate Jurisdiction, both as to Law and Fact, with such Exceptions, and under such Regulations as the Congress shall make.

The Trial of all Crimes, except in Cases of Impeachment, shall be by Jury; and such Trial shall be held in the State where the said Crimes shall have been committed; but when not committed within any State, the Trial shall be at such Place or Places as the Congress may by Law have directed.

SECTION. 3. Treason against the United States, shall consist only in levying War against them, or in adhering to their Enemies, giving them Aid and Comfort. No Person shall be convicted of Treason unless on the Testimony of two Witnesses to the same overt Act, or on Confession in open Court.

The Congress shall have Power to declare the Punishment of Treason, but no Attainder of Treason shall work Corruption of Blood, or Forfeiture except during the Life of the Person attainted.

Article. IV.

SECTION. 1. Full Faith and Credit shall be given in each State to the public Acts, Records, and judicial Proceedings of every other State. And the Congress may by general Laws prescribe the Manner in which such Acts, Records and Proceedings shall be proved, and the Effect thereof.

SECTION. 2. The Citizens of each State shall be entitled to all

---

* Modified by the Eleventh Amendment.

Privileges and Immunities of Citizens in the several States.

A Person charged in any State with Treason, Felony, or other Crime, who shall flee from Justice, and be found in another State, shall on Demand of the executive Authority of the State from which he fled, be delivered up, to be removed to the State having Jurisdiction of the Crime.

No Person held to Service or Labour in one State, under the Laws thereof, escaping into another, shall, in Consequence of any Law or Regulation therein, be discharged from such Service or Labour, but shall be delivered up on Claim of the Party to whom such Service or Labour may be due.

SECTION. 3. New States may be admitted by the Congress into this Union; but no new State shall be formed or erected within the Jurisdiction of any other State, nor any State be formed by the Junction of two or more States, or Parts of States, without the Consent of the Legislatures of the States concerned as well as of the Congress.

The Congress shall have Power to dispose of and make all needful Rules and Regulations respecting the Territory or other Property belonging to the United States; and nothing in this Constitution shall be so construed as to Prejudice any Claims of the United States, or of any particular State.

SECTION. 4. The United States shall guarantee to every State in this Union a Republican Form of Government, and shall protect each of them against Invasion; and on Application of the Legislature, or of the Executive (when the Legislature cannot be convened) against domestic Violence.

Article. V.

The Congress, whenever two thirds of both Houses shall deem it necessary, shall propose Amendments to this Constitution, or, on the Application of the Legisiatures of two thirds of the several States, shall call a Convention for proposing Amendments, which, in either Case, shall be valid to all Intents and Purposes, as Part of this Constitution, when ratified by the Legislatures of three fourths of the several States, or by Conventions in three fourths thereof, as the one or the other Mode of Ratification may be proposed by the Congress; Provided that no Amendment which may be made prior to the Year One thousand eight hundred and eight shall in any Manner affect the first and fourth Clauses in the Ninth Section of the first Article; and that no State, without its Consent, shall be deprived of it's equal Suffrage in the Senate.

Article. VI.

All Debts contracted and Engagements entered into, before the Adoption of this Constitution, shall be as valid against the United States under this Constitution, as under the Confederation.

This Constitution, and the Laws of the United States which shall be made in Pursuance thereof; and all Treaties made, or which shall be made, under the Authority of the United States, shall be the supreme Law of the Land; and the Judges in every State shall be bound thereby, any Thing in the Constitution or Laws of any State to the Contrary notwithstanding.

The Senators and Representatives before mentioned, and the Members of the several State Legislatures, and all executive and judicial Officers, both of the United States and of the several States, shall be bound by Oath or Affirmation, to support this Constitution; but no religious Test shall ever be required as a Qualification to any Office or public Trust under the United States.

Article. VII.

The Ratification of the Conventions of nine States, shall be sufficient for the Establishment of this Constitution between the States so ratifying the Same.

done in Convention by the Unanimous Consent of the States present the Seventeenth Day of September in the Year of our Lord one thousand seven hundred and Eighty seven and of the Independance of the United States of America the Twelfth. **In witness** whereof We have hereunto subscribed our Names,

Articles in Addition to, and Amendment of, the Constitution of the United States of America, Proposed by Congress, and Ratified by the Legislatures of the Several States, Pursuant to the Fifth Article of the Original Constitution.

THE CONSTITUTION OF THE UNITED STATES

Amendment I*

Congress shall make no law respecting an establishment of religion, or prohibiting the free exercise thereof; or abridging the freedom of speech, or of the press; or the right of the people peaceably to assemble, and to petition the Government for a redress of grievances.

Amendment II

A well regulated Militia, being necessary to the security of a free State, the right of the people to keep and bear Arms shall not be infringed.

Amendment III

No Soldier shall, in time of peace, be quartered in any house, without the consent of the Owner, nor in time of war, but in a manner to be prescribed by law.

Amendment IV

The right of the people to be secure in their persons, houses, papers, and effects, against unreasonable searches and seizures, shall not be violated, and no Warrants shall issue, but upon probable cause, supported by Oath or affirmation, and particularly describing the place to be searched, and the persons or things to be seized.

Amendment V

No person shall be held to answer for a capital or otherwise infamous crime, unless on a presentment or indictment of a Grand Jury, except in cases arising in the land or naval forces, or in the Militia, when in actual service in time of War or public danger; nor shall any person be subject for the same offence to be twice put in jeopardy of life or limb; nor shall be compelled in any

---

* The first ten amendments were passed by Congress September 25, 1789. They were ratified by three-fourths of the states December 15, 1791.

criminal case to be a witness against himself, nor be deprived of life, liberty, or property, without due process of law; nor shall private property be taken for public use, without just compensation.

Amendment VI

In all criminal prosecutions, the accused shall enjoy the right to a speedy and public trial, by an impartial jury of the State and district wherein the crime shall have been committed, which district shall have been previously ascertained by law, and to be informed of the nature and cause of the accusation; to be confronted with the witnesses against him; to have compulsory process for obtaining witnesses in his favor, and to have the Assistance of Counsel for his defence.

Amendment VII

In suits at common law, where the value in controversy shall exceed twenty dollars, the right of trial by jury shall be preserved, and no fact tried by a jury, shall be otherwise reexamined in any Court of the United States, than according to the rules of the common law.

Amendment VIII

Excessive bail shall not be required, nor excessive fines imposed, nor cruel and unusual punishments inflicted.

Amendment IX

The enumeration in the Constitution, of certain rights, shall not be construed to deny or disparage others retained by the people.

THE CONSTITUTION OF THE UNITED STATES

Amendment X

The powers not delegated to the United States by the Constitution; nor prohibited by it to the States, are reserved to the States respectively, or to the people.

Amendment XI*

The Judicial power of the United States shall not be construed to extend to any suit in law or equity, commenced or prosecuted against one of the United States by Citizens of another State, or by Citizens or Subjects of any Foreign State.

Amendment XII†

The Electors shall meet in their respective States and vote by ballot for President and Vice-President, one of whom, at least, shall not be an inhabitant of the same State with themselves; they shall name in their ballots the person voted for as President, and in distinct ballots the person voted for as Vice-President, and they shall make distinct lists of all persons voted for as President, and of all persons voted for as Vice-President, and of the number of votes for each, which lists they shall sign and certify, and transmit sealed to the seat of the government of the United States, directed to the President of the Senate;—The President of the Senate shall, in the presence of the Senate and House of Representatives, open all the certificates and the votes shall then be counted;—The person having the greatest number of votes for President, shall be the President, if such number be a majority of the whole number of Electors appointed; and if no person have such majority, then from the persons having the highest numbers not exceeding three on the list of those voted for as President, the House of Representatives shall choose immediately, by ballot, the President. But in choosing the President, the votes shall be taken by states, the representation from each state having one vote; a quorum for this purpose shall consist of a member or members from two-thirds of the states, and a majority of all the states shall be necessary to

---

* Passed March 4, 1794. Ratified January 23, 1795.
† Passed December 9, 1803. Ratified June 15, 1804.

THE CONSTITUTION OF THE UNITED STATES

a choice. And if the House of Representatives shall not choose a President whenever the right of choice shall devolve upon them, before the fourth day of March next following, then the Vice-President shall act as President, as in the case of the death or other constitutional disability of the President.—The person having the greatest number of votes as Vice-President, shall be the Vice-President, if such number be a majority of the whole number of Electors appointed, and if no person have a majority, then from the two highest numbers on the list, the Senate shall choose the Vice-President; a quorum for the purpose shall consist of two-thirds of the whole number of Senators, and a majority of the whole number shall be necessary to a choice. But no person constitutionally ineligible to the office of President shall be eligible to that of Vice-President of the United States.

Amendment XIII*

SECTION 1. Neither slavery nor involuntary servitude, except as a punishment for crime whereof the party shall have been duly convicted, shall exist within the United States, or any place subject to their jurisdiction.

SECTION 2. Congress shall have power to enforce this article by appropriate legislation.

Amendment XIV†

SECTION 1. All persons born or naturalized in the United States, and subject to the jurisdiction thereof, are citizens of the United States and of the State wherein they reside. No State shall make or enforce any law which shall abridge the privileges or immunities of citizens of the United States; nor shall any State deprive any person of life, liberty, or property, without due process of law; nor deny to any person within its jurisdiction the equal protection of the laws.

SECTION 2. Representatives shall be apportioned among the several States according to their respective numbers, counting

---

* Passed January 31, 1865. Ratified December 6, 1865.
† Passed June 13, 1866. Ratified July 9, 1868.

160

THE CONSTITUTION OF THE UNITED STATES

the whole number of persons in each State, excluding Indians not taxed. But when the right to vote at any election for the choice of electors for President and Vice-President of the United States, Representatives in Congress, the Executive and Judicial officers of a State, or the members of the Legislature thereof, is denied to any of the male inhabitants of such State, being twenty-one years of age, and citizens of the United States, or in any way abridged, except for participation in rebellion, or other crime, the basis of representation therein shall be reduced in the proportion which the number of such male citizens shall bear to the whole number of male citizens twenty-one years of age in such State.

SECTION 3. No person shall be a Senator or Representative in Congress, or elector of President and Vice-President, or hold any office, civil or military, under the United States, or under any State, who, having previously taken an oath, as a member of Congress, or as an officer of the United States, or as a member of any State legislature, or as an executive or judicial officer of any State, to support the Constitution of the United States, shall have engaged in insurrection or rebellion against the same, or given aid or comfort to the enemies thereof. But Congress may by a vote of two-thirds of each House, remove such disability.

SECTION 4. The validity of the public debt of the United States, authorized by law, including debts incurred for payment of pensions and bounties for services in suppressing insurrection or rebellion, shall not be questioned. But neither the United States nor any State shall assume or pay any debt or obligation incurred in aid of insurrection or rebellion against the United States, or any claim for the loss or emancipation of any slave; but all such debts, obligations, and claims shall be held illegal and void.

SECTION 5. The Congress shall have the power to enforce, by appropriate legislation, the provisions of this article.

Amendment XV*

SECTION 1. The right of citizens of the United States to vote shall not be denied or abridged by the United States or by any State

---

* Passed February 26, 1869. Ratified February 2, 1870.

on account of race, color, or previous condition of servitude—
SECTION 2. The Congress shall have power to enforce this article
by appropriate legislation.

*Amendment XVI**

The Congress shall have power to lay and collect taxes on incomes, from whatever source derived, without apportionment
among the several States, and without regard to any census or
enumeration.

Amendment XVII†

The Senate of the United States shall be composed of two Senators
from each State, elected by the people thereof, for six years; and
each Senator shall have one vote. The electors in each State shall
have the qualifications requisite for electors of the most numerous
branch of the State legislatures.

When vacancies happen in the representation of any State in
the Senate, the executive authority of such State shall issue writs
of election to fill such vacancies: *Provided,* That the legislature
of any State may empower the executive thereof to make temporary appointments until the people fill the vacancies by election
as the legislature may direct.

This amendment shall not be so construed as to affect the election or term of any Senator chosen before it becomes valid as part
of the Constitution.

Amendment XVIII‡

SECTION 1. After one year from the ratification of this article
the manufacture, sale, or transportation of intoxicating liquors
within, the importation thereof into, or the exportation thereof
from the United States and all territory subject to the jurisdiction
thereof for beverage purposes is hereby prohibited.

---

* Passed July 12, 1909. Ratified February 3, 1913.
† Passed May 13, 1912. Ratified April 8, 1913.
‡ Passed December 18, 1917. Ratified January, 16, 1919.

THE CONSTITUTION OF THE UNITED STATES

SECTION 2. The Congress and the several States shall have concurrent power to enforce this article by appropriate legislation.
SECTION 3. This article shall be inoperative unless it shall have been ratified as an amendment to the Constitution by the legislatures of the several States, as provided in the Constitution, within seven years from the date of the submission hereof to the States by the Congress.

Amendment XIX*

The right of citizens of the United States to vote shall not be denied or abridged by the United States or by any State on account of sex.

Congress shall have power to enforce this article by appropriate legislation.

Amendment XX†

SECTION 1. The terms of the President and Vice-President shall end at noon on the 20th day of January, and the terms of Senators and Representatives at noon on the 3d day of January, of the years in which such terms would have ended if this article had not been ratified; and the terms of their successors shall then begin.
SECTION 2. The Congress shall assemble at least once in every year, and such meeting shall begin at noon on the 3d day of January, unless they shall by law appoint a different day.
SECTION 3. If, at the time fixed for the beginning of the term of the President, the President elect shall have died, the Vice-President elect shall become President. If a President shall not have been chosen before the time fixed for the beginning of his term, or if the President elect shall have failed to qualify, then the Vice-President elect shall act as President until a President shall have qualified; and the Congress may by law provide for the case wherein neither a President elect nor a Vice-President elect shall have qualified, declaring who shall then act as Presi-

---

* Passed June 4, 1919. Ratified August 18, 1920.
† Passed March 2, 1932. Ratified January 23, 1933.

dent, or the manner in which one who is to act shall be selected, and such person shall act accordingly until a President or Vice-President shall have qualified.

SECTION 4. The Congress may by law provide for the case of the death of any of the persons from whom the House of Representatives may choose a President whenever the right of choice shall have devolved upon them, and for the case of the death of any of the persons from whom the Senate may choose a Vice-President whenever the right of choice shall have devolved upon them.

SECTION 5. Sections 1 and 2 shall take effect on the 15th day of October following the ratification of this article.

SECTION 6. This article shall be inoperative unless it shall have been ratified as an amendment to the Constitution by the legislatures of three-fourths of the several States within seven years from the date of its submission.

*Amendment XXI**

SECTION 1. The eighteenth article of amendment to the Constitution of the United States is hereby repealed.

SECTION 2. The transportation or importation into any State, Territory, or possession of the United States for delivery or use therein of intoxicating liquors, in violation of the laws thereof, is hereby prohibited.

SECTION 3. This article shall be inoperative unless it shall have been ratified as an amendment to the Constitution by conventions in the several States, as provided in the Constitution, within seven years from the date of the submission hereof to the States by the Congress.

Amendment XXII†

No person shall be elected to the office of the President more than twice, and no person who has held the office of President, or acted as President, for more than two years of a term to which some other person was elected President shall be elected to the office of the President more than once.

---

* Passed February 20, 1933. Ratified December 5, 1933.

† Passed March 12, 1947. Ratified March 1, 1951.

164

THE CONSTITUTION OF THE UNITED STATES

But this Article shall not apply to any person holding the office of President when this Article was proposed by the Congress, and shall not prevent any person who may be holding the office of President, or acting as President, during the term within which this Article becomes operative from holding the office of President or acting as President during the remainder of such term.

Amendment XXIII*

SECTION 1. The District constituting the seat of Government of the United States shall appoint in such manner as the Congress may direct:

A number of electors of President and Vice President equal to the whole number of Senators and Representatives in Congress to which the District would be entitled if it were a State, but in no event more than the least populous State; they shall be in addition to those appointed by the States, but they shall be considered, for the purposes of the election of President and Vice President, to be electors appointed by the State; and they shall meet in the District and perform such duties as provided by the twelfth article of amendment.

SECTION 2. The Congress shall have power to enforce this article by appropriate legislation.

Amendment XXIV†

SECTION 1. The right of citizens of the United States to vote in any primary or other election for President or Vice President, or for Senator or Representative in Congress, shall not be denied or abridged by the United States or any State by reason of failure to pay any poll tax or other tax.

SECTION 2. The Congress shall have power to enforce this article by appropriate legislation.

---

* Passed June 16, 1960. Ratified April 3, 1961.
† Passed August 27, 1962. Ratified January 23, 1964.

Amendment XXV*

SECTION 1. In case of the removal of the President from office or of his death or resignation, the Vice President shall become President.

SECTION 2. Whenever there is a vacancy in the office of the Vice President, the President shall nominate a Vice President who shall take office upon confirmation by a majority vote of both Houses of Congress.

SECTION 3. Whenever the President transmits to the President pro tempore of the Senate and the Speaker of the House of Representatives his written declaration that he is unable to discharge the powers and duties of his office, and until he transmits to them a written declaration to the contrary, such powers and duties shall be discharged by the Vice President as Acting President.

SECTION 4. Whenever the Vice President and a majority of either the principal officers of the executive department or of such other body as Congress may by law provide, transmit to the President pro tempore of the Senate and the Speaker of the House of Representatives their written declaration that the President is unable to discharge the powers and duties of his office, the Vice President shall immediately assume the powers and duties of the office of Acting President.

Thereafter, when the President transmits to the President pro tempore of the Senate and the Speaker of the House of Representatives his written declaration that no inability exists, he shall resume the powers and duties of his office unless the Vice President and a majority of either the principal officers of the executive department or of such other body as Congress may by law provide, transmit within four days to the President pro tempore of the Senate and the Speaker of the House of Representatives their written declaration that the President is unable to discharge the powers and duties of his office. Thereupon Congress shall decide the issue, assembling within forty-eight hours for that purpose if not in session. If the Congress, within twenty-

---

* Passed July 6, 1965. Ratified February 11, 1967.

one days after receipt of the latter written declaration, or, if Congress is not in session, within twenty-one days after Congress is required to assemble, determines by two-thirds vote of both Houses that the President is unable to discharge the powers and duties of his office, the Vice President shall continue to discharge the same as Acting President; otherwise, the President shall resume the powers and duties of his office.

*Amendment XXVI**

SECTION 1. The right of citizens of the United States, who are eighteen years of age or older, to vote shall not be denied or abridged by the United States or by any State on account of age. SECTION 2. The Congress shall have power to enforce this article by appropriate legislation.

PROPOSED *Amendment XXVII*†

SECTION 1. Equality of rights under the law shall not be denied or abridged by the United States or by any State on account of sex. SECTION 2. The Congress shall have the power to enforce, by appropriate legislation, the provisions in this Article.

---

* Passed March 23, 1971. Ratified July 5, 1971.
† Passed March 24, 1972. Ratified ?

Bibliography

Abraham, Henry J., *Freedom and the Court: Civil Rights and Liberties in the United States.* New York: Oxford University Press, 1967. (paper)

Asch, Sidney H., *Civil Rights and Responsibilities Under the Constitution.* New York: Arco, 1968.

Cahn, Edmond, ed., *The Great Rights.* New York: Macmillan, 1963.

Cummings, Milton C., Jr., and Wise, David, *Democracy Under Pressure: An Introduction to the American Political System.* New York: Harcourt Brace Jovanovich, 1971.

Douglas, William O., *A Living Bill of Rights.* New York: Doubleday, 1961.

Goodman, Elaine and Walter, *The Rights of the People: The Major Decisions of the Warren Court.* New York: Farrar, Straus and Giroux, 1971.

Hall, Livingston, and Kamisar, Yale, *Modern Criminal Procedure.* St. Paul: West Publishing Co., 1966.

Hunt, Morton, *The Mugging.* New York: Atheneum, 1972.

168

BIBLIOGRAPHY

Lewis, Anthony, *Gideon's Trumpet*. New York: Vintage, 1964. (paper)

Lineberry, William P., ed., *Justice in America: Law, Order, and the Courts*. New York: H. W. Wilson, 1972.

McDonald, Forrest, *Enough Wise Men: The Story of Our Constitution*. New York: Putnam, 1970.

Morris, Richard B., *The American Revolution Reconsidered*. New York: Harper and Row, 1967.

Paine, Thomas, *The Complete Writings, Vol. I* (Collected and edited by Philip S. Foner, Ph.D.). New York: The Citadel Press, 1945.

Trevelyan, George O., *The American Revolution* (ed., Richard B. Morris). New York: David McKay, 1964.

Index